AFGHANISTAN, MONGOLIA AND USSR

BY THE SAME AUTHOR

Modern Nepal
Struggle for Central Asia
The Himalaya as a Frontier
Politics of Central Asia
Modern Bhutan
Government and Politics of Tibet and many others

AFGHANISTAN, MONGOLIA AND USSR

RAM RAHUL

VIKAS PUBLISHING HOUSE PVT LTD

VIKAS PUBLISHING HOUSE PVT LTD
576, Masjid Road, Jangpura, New Delhi-110014

COPYRIGHT © RAM RAHUL, 1987

All rights reserved. No part of this publication may be reproduced in any form without the prior written permission of the publishers.

Printed by:
Chetna Printers, A-27/2A, Shastri Marg, Maujpur, Delhi-110053

To My Parents
Maha Ram and Umrao Kaur
who enabled me to make my life
as I thought proper

PREFACE

Afghanistan, Mongolia and USSR concerns the political position, of Afghanistan and Mongolia since the 1920s when they rid themselves of the imperialist control of Britain and China respectively. It is a study of Afghanistan and Mongolia in world politics. It is a study of their political connection with the Union of Soviet Socialist Republics (USSR).

I first survey the political positions of Afghanistan and Mongolia up to the end of the world war in 1918 and then study the development of their special relations with the USSR from 1919 to 1986. It is fascinating to study how they began their careers as independent states, how they became British and Chinese dependencies, how they regained their independence from Britain and China and how they become dependencies of the USSR.

Both Afghanistan and Mongolia have a long history of geopolitical importance. Both are in the Soviet sphere now, but, owing to their geographical location between China, India, Iran, and USSR, both retain their importance in regional as well as international politics. The fact of their location has always affected their political status. Although small countries, they have always had big influence on their great neighbours, Russia/USSR, Iran, India and China.

Except for notes and references, *Afghanistan, Mongolia and USSR* has been written direct. There is no unnecessary lengthening of the study. The Appendices contain the first and last treaties between Afghanistan and the USSR and between Mongolia and the USSR especially to show the development of the political connection between them. The common contents of these treaties as well as their language is remarkable. The Bibliography contains sources in English, including translations of Chinese, Mongol, Persian and Russian works, since the end of the World War I. It contains books I have used as well as books of value for the modern history of Afghanistan and Mongolia even though I may not have used them. It does not contain works in languages such as French and German, although there are excellent volumes in these languages on both Afghanistan and Mongolia.

I hope my transliteration (romanization) of Afghan, Mongol and Russian names and terms is all right. All Chinese names and terms up to 1949, I have spelt according to the Wade-Giles system of transliteration of the Chinese language. After 1949, these have been spelt according to the Pinyin system.

I like to express my appreciation to my friends Girja Kumar, of Jawaharlal Nehru University (New Delhi) and R.P. Puri of Central News Agency (New Delhi) for their constant interest in my work on Central Asia. I am also thankful to Professors C.R. Bowden and M.E. Yapp of the School of Oriental and African Studies (London) who read pieces of the manuscript and made useful commects. Except myself, no body is responsible for the blemishes of this study.

RAM RAHUL

CONTENTS

	Preface	vii
1.	INTRODUCTION	1
2.	AFGHANISTAN 1919-1945	23
3.	AFGHANISTAN 1945-	33
4.	MONGOLIA 1921-1945	51
5.	MONGOLIA 1945-	59
6.	POSTFACE	73
	Appendix I	79
	Appendix II	86
	Bibliography	90
	Index	94

1

INTRODUCTION

Afghanistan and Mongolia are ancient lands of ancient peoples in the centre of Asia. The Scythians and the Greeks passed through Afghanistan, and the Huns and the Turks nomadized on the Mongol steppes. Both Afghanistan and Mongolia have played important roles in the history and politics of Asia. Both have ruled, and have been ruled from, China, India and Iran. At one time, from 1240 to 1480, the Mongols, even dominated Russia and campaigned further west. The Afghans, of course, never had any such connection with Russia. Today's Afghanistan and Mongolia are states of the Soviet system, and are members of the United Nations (UN). But what actually is their status ? A study of their present political connection with the Union of Soviet Socialist Republics (USSR) is of more than academic importance.

Ahmad Shah (1723-73) of the Sadozai clan of the Abdali, later Durrani, tribe created the political structure of modern Afghanistan at Kandahar in 1747. His domain extended from the Aral Sea to India. Britain, the sea power, and Russia, the land power, were yet to appear for the power game in Central and West Asia. That game began nearly a hundred years later. Britain and Russia then stood far apart in Asia. The British had only a few trading centres in India; the Russians had political bases only in the Caucasus and Ural territories.

The state authority of Afghanistan, which Ahmad Shah had established, disintegrated by 1818 mainly on account of the wars of succession among his grandsons (as well as the forces of external circumstances such as the extension of the power politics of Europe to Asia) by the 1800s. The Sadozais lost the throne of Afghanistan largely because of intra-clan discords. The assassination of *Sardar* (Chief)[1] Payinda Khan, son of Haji Jamal Khan of the powerful Barakzai clan of the Durrani tribe, destroyed the spirit of cooperation between the Barakzais and the Sadozais and led to a bitter feud between them, finally resulting in the division of the country. Sardar

Dost Muhammad Khan (1793-1863), youngest of Payinda Khan's many sons, eventually emerged supreme. When he ascended the throne of Kabul in 1826, he took the title *Amir*. He came to be known as the *Amir-i-Kabir*, the Great Amair.

At the turn of the century, the British apprehended a Napoleonic scheme to sabotage the British land route to India. The British also looked upon the Franco-Russian pact concluded by Emperor Napoleon I (1769-1831) and Tsar Aleksandr (*r.* 1801-25) at Tilsit on the Nieman River on 9 July 1807 as ominous. Russia's support of the claim of Persia to Herat alarmed the British, who looked upon Herat, because of its strategic location, as a barrier against the spread of Russian influence to Afghanistan. They believed that if India were to be secure, Herat must not become part of Persia. They interpreted the Russo-Persian treaty of friendship concluded in Turkmanchai, belonging to Tabriz, on 21 February 1828 to entitle Russia to post a consul at Herat in the event of its capture by Persia. Therefore, they viewed the capture of Herat by Persia with Russian help as leading to the establishment of Russian footing in Afghanistan. The position of Herat between Britain and Russia ultimately became the cause of a war between Afghanistan and the British government in India, the Anglo-Afghan war of 1839-1843.

The treaty concluded by Russia and Turkey in Adrianople on 2 December 1829 transformed the defence of India, according to the British, from a military to a political problem, from the fear of the invasion of India by Russia to the fear of the extension of the influence of Russia towards India.

To the British protest concerning the size of Russia's territorial acquisition in Asia under the the Russo-Ottoman treaty of 1829, Count Karl Nesselrode, foreign minister of Russia, said: "If by the annexation of several Ottoman cities ... Russia has broken the balance [of power] of Europe, the English government by its conquests in India has systematically been breaking it." Thus began the struggle between Britain and Russia for influence in West Asia, and Afghanistan. At this time both Britain and Russia were interested in Herat because of its strategic location.

Under the circumstances the British sided with Shah Shuja-ul-Mulk of the Sadozdi dynasty, a brother of Zaman Shah (*r.* 1793-1800), a son of Timur Shah (*r.*1773-93) and a grandson of Ahmad Shah, who had attempted to regain the throne of Afghanistan with the help of maharaja Ranjit Singh (1780-1839) of Panjab in 1833-34. They declared war against the principalities of Kabul and Kandahar on 1

Introduction 3

October 1839 alleging that Amir Dost Muhammad had made overtures to Persia and Russia. Shuja was then living in exile in Ludhiana in British India on a British stipend. Mountstuart Elphinstone had concluded with him at Peshawar, the winter capital of Afghanistan, in February 1809, a treaty of friendship and alliance to protect Afghanistan, but in actuality to protect the fledgling British dominion in India from the threat of Napoleon.

Before advancing on Afghanistan the British discussed numerous schemes for subverting the power of Amir Dost Muhammad, including the military intervention of Maharaja Ranjit Singh in Afghanistan (vide the treaty between the British, Maharaja Ranjit Singh and Shah Shuja, known as the triparite treaty of friendship and alliance of 23 July 1838, based on the treaty of 1833 between, Ranjit Singh and Shah Shuja). Fearing, however, that the intervention of Ranjit Singh might lead to his establishing himself at Kabul, the British did not invite him to join the military expedition to Afghanistan. Before his emergence as the Maharaja of Panjab, Ranjit Singh had been governor of Zaman Shah in Panjab from 1793 to 1799.

The British restored Shuja on the throne of Afghanistan in Kabul and deported Dost Muhammad to India. But they could not keep him on the throne for long. The British invasion of Afghanistan unwittingly united the Afghans, who ousted Shah Shuja from the throne and annihilated the British force in a disastrous retreat from Kabul in the spring of 1842. Sardar Sujauddola, son of Zaman Shah, assassinated Shah Shuja in Kabul on 15 April 1842. Dost Muhammad returned to the throne of Kabul in 1843.

The British disastrous defeat in, and withdrawal from, Afghanistan barred the British power from Afghanistan. The British realized that they could not achieve their objective of turning Afghanistan into a British protectorate so long as they were not masters of Panjab and Sindh. They had also known, since Mountstaast Elphinstone's mission to Shah Shuja in 1808-9, that a connection with Afghanistan could unite the Sikhs of Panjab and the Amirs of Sindh. Their annexation of Panjab and Sindh in 1849-50 advanced the British frontier from the Satluj River to the Indus River and made it contiguous to that of Afghanistan. The British frontier, the erstwhile Sikh frontier, passed between the Indus River and the foothills inhabited by the Pathan/Pashtun tribes on the fringes of the plains.

In view of the difficulties with Persia over Herat, Amir Dost Muhammad concluded with the British government in India a treaty of perpetual peace and friendship at Peshawar on 30 March 1855. By this treaty they agreed to respect each other's territories and never to interfere therein. Dost Muhammad specially engaged himself "to be the friend of the friends and enemy of the enemies of the Honourable East India Company". He remained true to the treaty of 1855 even though the Pathan/Pashtun tribesmen hailed the revolt of 1857 in India. He unified Afghanistan. He brought all the *cis*-Amu Darya/ Oxus River Uzbek principalities of West Turkistan under his rule in a series of military campaigns. He was even able to take Herat just before his death in 1863. Sardar Sher Ali Khan (1821-79), who succeeded his father Amir Dost Muhammad, further consolidated Afghanistan.

Amir Sher Ali endeavoured to reach an agreement with the British government of India for help in the event of Russian aggression against Afghanistan. The capture of Tashkent in 1865 and the annexation of Samarkand in 1869 by Russi established Russian power at the Amu Darya for the first time. Russian expansion in Central Asia posed a political problem for the British. The British government of India, however, ignored Amir Sher Ali's quest for British protection and also his desire for the acceptance of his younger son, Abdullah Jan, who had accompanied him to Ambala in India in the spring of 1869 to meet Lord Mayo, viceroy and governor general of India from 1869 to 1872, as his *Vali Ahad*, heir apparent and successor to the throne of Afghanistan. (Abdullah Jan died on 17 August 1878.) The British award over the Sistan boundary between Afghanistan and Persia in 1872 was another point of discord between Amir Sher Ail and the British. Under the award of 1872 Sistan went to Persia, and outer Sistan to Afghanistan and Baluchistan. Thus the award was favourable to Persia. The Sistan boundary question continued to strain relations between Afghanistan and Persia/Iran[2] up to mid 1974.

Under the circumstances, Amir Sher Ail turned to Russia. A Russian mission, led by General G.N. Stoletov, visited Kabul, where Amir Sher Ali received them on 22 July 1878. General Stoletov drew up with Amir Sher Ail a draft treaty which guaranteed the independence of Afghanistan and promised Russian non-interference in its internal affairs. The Russian government recalled the Stoletov mission a week before the closing of the Congress of Berlin, which had been convened as a consequence of the Russo-Turkish War of 1877-1978 in which Russia had been victorious. According to the British, Russia dispatched the Stoletov mission in order to obtain British concessions relating to the Ottoman Empire after the Russo-Turkish

War Russia perhaps sent it in retaliation for the British action (Russia's humiliation) at the Congress of Berlin on 13 June 1878. The Tsar bitterly spoke of this Congress as the European coalition against Russia under the leadership of Prince Bismark. As an independent ruler, Amir Sher Ali had every right to receive or reject any mission, whether British or Russian. Anyway his reception of the Russian mission earned him the displeasure of Lord Lytton, viceroy and governor general of India from 1876 to 1880, who used it as a pretext to intervene in Afghanistan. Britain's concern then, as also later, was not only to preserve Afghanistan from Russian influence but also to limit Russia to the north of the Amu Darya and defend India as far north as possible. Before the Anglo-Afghan War of 1839-43, the British effort had been to halt the advance of Russia to the east of the Caspian Sea.

Amir Sher Ali abdicated in favour of his elder son, Sardar Yakub Khan, and escaped to North Afghanistan. He died at Mazar-i-Sharif on 21 February 1879. The British accepted Sardar Yakub Khan as the Amir of Afghanistan. Sardar Ayub Khan, Amir Sher Ali's other son, was governor of Herat then.

The Anglo-Afghan War of 1878-79, an attempt to forestall and hold back Russia from Afghanistan, was the result of the British failure to make a proper diplomatic arrangement with Amir Sher Ali. In the 1860s and 1870s, as in the 1830s, the British were nervous about Russian advance in Central Asia. They suffered early losses, but eventually won. The Anglo-Afghan peace treaty signed in Gandamak on 26 May 1879 provided for the control of the external affairs of Afghanistan by the British government of India and their pledge of non-interference in the internal affairs of Afghanistan. The British also acquired the strategic frontier areas of Kurram, Pishin and Sibi as well as the famous Khaibar/Khyber Pass. They absorbed Baluchistan into their Indian Empire. They had taken Kalat, capital of Baluchistan, in 1872.

The Afghans, who united in this critical juncture, killed the British agent in the Bala Hisar of Kabul on 3 December 1879. Sardar Abdur Rahman Khan (1844-1901), a son of Sardar Muhammad Afzal Khan[3] and a nephew of Amir Sher Ali, returned from a long exile in Samarkand (Russia). He had gone there in protest against his father's sending a letter of allegiance to Amir Sher Ali. He won the throne of Afghanistan on 22 July 1880. Some of the chiefs of Afghanistan continued in their loyalty to the widow and sons of Amir Sher Ali. But Amir Abdur Rahman successfully conciliated them.

Sardar Ayub Khan escaped to Mashhad in Persia, eventually to Rawalpindi and Lahore in India. The erstwhile Amir Yakub settled at Mussoorie in India on a British stipend.

Sardar Ayub Khan routed a British force at Maiwand near Kandahar on 27 July 1880. To commemorate the victory of Maiwand, Kabul built several monuments and pillars during the reign of King Zahir Shah. It named the main avenue of Kabul as Jada-i-Maiwand, and the Chardeh residential area as Ghazi Ayub Khan Karta. Kabul also commemorated the memory of the young Pashtun heroine Malalai, who encouraged the fighting men in this battle by waving her *chadri* (veil) as a flag and by singing an inspiring Pashtu couplet, by naming a hospital for women and girls in her honour.

The British, who accepted Sardar Abdur Rahman as the Amir of Afghanistan in spite of his exile of eleven years in Central Asia on a Russian stipend, handed over Kandahar to him on 21 April 1881. Amir Abdur Rahman accepted the Anglo-Afghan treaty of 1879 which had established the British protectorate over Afghanistan. He reconfirmed his agreement in 1893. The British jealously guarded their right to control Afghanistan against influence from other powers, particularly Russia, thereby imposing a heavy price for their pledge of non-interference in Afghanistan's internal affairs. The British government of India appointed its first native agent at Kabul in the summer of 1882. It conferred the title of GCSI (Grand Commander of the Order of the Star of India) on Amir Abdur Rahman. The Amir never used this insignia.

A formidable autocrat, Amir Abdur Rahman strengthened his authority by institutionalizing the royal succession, the civil bureaucracy and the army. He organized Afghanistan into provinces and districts. He pacified both the Pathan/Pashtun and non-Pathan/Pashtun tribes of Afghanistan or managed to keep their power under control. The Pathan/Pashtun tribes, the major tribes of Afghanistan, have always played a crucial role in the politics of Afghanistan. For example, the Mahsuds and the Wazirs overthrew King Amanullah in the civil war of the *Bacha-i-Saqqa* (son of water carrier), a one-eyed Tajik brigand named Habibullah, in 1929. Among the non-Afghan tribes such as the Baluch, Hazara, Tajik, Turkmen and Uzbek tribes, Abdur Rahman smashed the rebellion of the Hazaras and Khilzais.

Several Pashtun dignitaries such as the brothers Sardar Asif Khan and Sardar Yusuf Khan, sons of Sardar Yahya Khan and nephews of Abdur Rahman, went into exile in India. Their sons, all born in India, played historic roles in the Anglo-Afghan War of 1919 and the Civil War of 1929.

Lord Dufferin, viceroy and governor general of India from 1884 to 1888, formally invited and personally received Amir Abdur Rahman at the frontier post of Zamrud at the mouth of the Khybar Pass in the spring of 1885. On 29 March 1885 Russia claimed Panjdeh, including the Zulfiqar Pass, as within the area which had passed into its control after its capture and occupation of Merv in western Central Asia. The British government considered Panjdeh as part of Afghanistan and its occupation by Russia as a threat to Herat. In the face of the British resentment of the Russian occupation of Panjdeh, an Anglo-Russian war over the question of the right to possess Panjdeh was imminent.

The British promised Abdur Rahman that it would prevent the seizure of Herat by Russia. However, Abdur Rahman, who was visiting Rawalpindi at the time of the Russian advance, declared that he was not sure whether Panjdeh really belonged to Afghanistan, and that securing the Zulfiqar Pass lying between Panjdeh and Herat would satisfy him. We do not really know if the Amir pronounced himself unwilling to go to war for Panjdeh. Or was it the subtle diplomacy of N.K. Giers, the then foreign minister of Russia, that averted the war. Whatever it might have been, an Anglo-Russian conflict over Panjdeh would necessarilly have harmed Afghanistan. The Anglo-Russian protocol of 1887, ending the crisis over the border dispute by diplomacy, ceded Panjdeh to Russia and the Zulfiqar Pass to Afghanistan.

Amir Abdur Rahman secured for Afghanistan definitive boundaries which had been in flux. Up to the time of Amir Yakub, Amir Abdur Rahman's erstwhile precedessor, the country had no firm boundaries. The Durand Line (named after Sir Mortimer Durand, foreign secretary of the government of Iadia, who had led the delegation for talks between Afghanistan and India) agreement signed in Kabul on 12 November 1893 assigned the Pathans/Pashtuns to both Afghanistan and India. The unfortunate consequences of the Durand award are dogging Afghanistan even in its present travails. The Anglo-Russian Pamir boundary commission ceded vide the agreement signed in January 1895, Badakhshan and the narrow strip of Wakhan to Afghanistan mainly to secure a viable line of separation between the British and Russian empires in the Pamir region. The inconvenience of a Russian wedge driven between Afghnistan and China and touching the passes, which lie to the north of the frontier principalities of Chitral, Hunza and Nagar, was too obvious to the British. The government of India established, in 1889, a political agency at Gilgit both to keep an eye on Chitral, Hunza and Nagar as well as to guard the frontier with Russia. The British even examined the feasibility of the division of the Pamir region between Afghanistan and China. They wanted to keep the Russians as far away from the Pamir mountains as possible. They were against any gap which might enable the Russians to intrude into the Hindu Kush region.

To begin with, Amir Abdur Rahman was reluctant to take Wakhan into Afghanistan and hold it. But the offer of the British subsidy (the standard British device at that time) of more than Rs 1,000,000 annually was perhaps irresistible.

Although Amir Abdur Rahman was more tolerant of the British than of the Russian influence in his country, he sought to pursue a policy of balance between the expanding British and Russian empires : Afghanistan's independence and security depended on such a policy. He set forth the advantages of such a policy thus :

On both sides of Afghanistan there powerful neighbours namely England and Russia. Though these neighbours are the cause of much anxiety to Afghanistan, yet, as they are pulling against each other, they are no less an advantage and protection for Afghanistan than a danger. Indeed a great deal of the safety of the Afghan Government depends upon the fact that neither of these neighbours can bear to allow the other to annex an inch of Afghan territory.

He was quite wary of the British intentions towards his country. For, decade after decade, the British deployed a large army, a force of 70,000 troops on active service in the North-West Frontier of India and kept 70,000 troops in reserve at Lahore and Delhi. To the British, the Russians, masters of western Central Asia, were a threat to India's security.

Sardar Habibullah Khan (1872-1919), eldest son of Amir Abdur Rahman, succeeded his father after the lather's death on 2 October 1901. His succession on 3 October took place without any upheaval, a rare occurrence in the polygamous society of Afghanistan. Apparently the strong hand of his father had put an end to royal family intransigencies and quarrels.

In 1903 Amir Habibullah proclaimed an amnesty in favour of all Afghans, including the families of the Barakzai and Sadozai royal clans, banished by his father in the 1880s. This lightened the harshness of the measures enforced by his father. Amir Habibullah's gesture led to the return of a large number of Afghans such as the family of Mahmud Tarzi, from India, Persia, Turkey and Central Asia, to Afghanistan. The families of Amir Yaqub and Sardar Ayub Khan and a number of the sardars of Kandahar ignored the amnesty. Most of them returned to Afghanistan in the 1930s.

Also in 1903, Amir Habibullah established the first modern school for boys in Afghanistan, naming it Habibiya (now Habibiya High School) after his own name. Later, the reorganization of its curriculum introduced the teaching of subjects other than theology. When the Amir visited India from 2 January to 7 March 1907 on the invitation of the government of India, he selected in Aligarh teachers for his Habibiya school. In 1905 the Amir encouraged the establishment of the Sirajul Akhbar Association and the publication of the *Sirajul Akhbar-i-Afghanyia*.[4] Above all, he gave Afghanistan its national flag.

Amir Habibullah pursued the foreign policy of his father. On 21 1905 he signed an agreement with the government of India confirming the commitment of his father and affirming the treaty of 1893. However, he did not give his consent to the Anglo-Russian convention, concluded in Moscow on 31 August 1907, to divide his country into their spheres of influence. The government of Afghanistan, like the government of Persia, protested against it which had been concluded without its knowledge.

Amir Habibullah remained neutral during the world war of 1914-1918 in spite of pressure from the German-Turkish mission and from Indian revolutionaries such as Mohammed Barkatullah and Mahendra Pratap and from fervent Afghan nationalists to support the Central Powers particularly Germany against the Allies particularly Britain. The German-Turkish mission, which was in Kabul in 1915-16, was a venture to foment trouble along the frontier of Afghanistan with India during the war.

Sardar Amanullah Khan (1892-1960), youngest son of Amir Habibullah, succeeded his father on the latter's assassination in Jalalabad on 21 February 1919. From the very beginning he sought to terminate British control of Afghanistan. In March he let the British Viceroy of India know that he had unilaterally annulled all treaties and agreements imposed on Afghanistan by the Brrtish. He proclaimed Afghanistan an independent country. He changed the policy of his forebears, his father Amir Habibullah and his grandfather Amir Abdur Rahman. He initiated relations with other powers particularly with the newly created revolutionary regime in Russia. He created the ministry of foreign affairs of Afghanistan, and appointed his father-in-law Mahmud Tarzi foreign minister.

On 3 May 1919 Amir Amanullah declared a *Jihad* (holy war) against the British. *Sipah Salar* (General) Sardar Mohammed Nadir Khan (1883-1933) emerged as a hero from the short war which ended on 8 August 1919. On his side, he had his brothers Sardar Mohammed Ali Khan (d. 1920), Sardar Mohammed Aziz Khan (d. 1933), Sardar Mohammed Hashim Khan (1884-1953), Sardar Shah Mahmud Khan (1890-1959), and Sardar Shah Wali Khan (1885-1977) and cousins Sardar Mohammed Sulaiman Khan and Sardar Ali Ahmad Khan sons of Sardar Muhammad Asif Khan and Sardar Muhammad Yusuf Khan, who had returned to Afghanistan from India with their families during the reign of Amir Abdur Rahman.

The Afghans neither lost nor won the month long war in military terms. However, they erected a monument to commemorate it, called it a victory monument and put up a lion in chains—the lion representing British power. The British, though militarily triumphant, agreed to Afghanistan's control of its own foreign affairs. The peace treaty signed by the Afghans and the British in Rawalpindi (India) on 8 August 1919 conceded the independence of Afghanistan. Of course, the British tried to keep control over Afghanistan by reserving the right to limit Afghanistan's imports of arms and ammunition.

Thus, at the end of the world war of 1914-1918, Afghanistan had shaken off the grip of western imperialism and emerged as an independent nation. Amir Amanullah terminated the alliance with Britain, because it made Afghanistan a dependency and circumscribed the options of the Afghans to safeguard their national interests.

The Mongols, descendants of the Huns, were powerful neighbours of China in ancient times. To prevent them from entering into their country, the Chinese built defence fortifications, later linked to form the famous Great Wall of China, along their northern frontiers. To maintain peace they even arranged marriages between members of their royal family and the chiefs of the Hun tribes, called Xiangnu by the Chinese. However, the world first became aware of the Mongols only in the thirteenth century, when Temujin (1162—1227) led his tribe in conquering most of the other Mongol tribes and creating a unified Mongol state.

Temujin gained recognition of his power and position through his election as *Chinggis Khan* (Great Emperor) in 1020/1206 by a *quriltai* (assembly) of his family and supporters convened at the headwaters of the Onon River. Teb Tengri, the Mongol shaman, who presided over Temujin's rise to power, conferred upon him the title *Chinggis*

Khan. Indeed Temunjin is best know in history by his title of Chinggis Khan

Unification enabled the Mongols to proceed to the conquest of China, Afghanistan, Iran and Russia. The Mongols campaigned even in Burma, Korea and Japan and went up to Srivijaya in Sumatra (which is now part of Indonesia) in the east and Poland in the west. Chinggis Khan thus ruled one of the greatest land empires. His heirs extended it from the Pacific Ocean in the east to the Black See in the west and from Siberia in the north to India in the south. There was yet no Japan or Russia, as later in the nineteenth and twentieth centuries, for rivalry for supermacy in East Asia. Khubilai Khan (1216-96), a grandson of Chinggis Khan, established the Mongol Yuan dynasty of China. He made Peking his capital in 1260.

On the fall of the Mongol Empire (Toghon Temur *Ukhaghtu Khan*, last Mongol emperor of China who was known as Shun Ti) and the retreat of the Mongols into their ancestral lands, Mongol unity disappeared even on the Mongol steppes. However, under the heirs of Chinggis Khan, Mongolia managed to maintain its indpendence in the face of challenges from the Ming dynasty of China as well as its independent relations with Russia and Tibet from the fourteenth to the seventeenth centuries. The Mings could not vanquish the freedom-loving spirit of the Mongols. Ligdan Khan 1592—1634), the Khan of the Chahar Mongols, was the last great khan of all Mongols.

The Manchus occupied the territory held by the southern, Chahar Mongols by 1634. They turned their attention to the northern, Khalkha Mongols and the western, Oirat Mongols only after the complete pacification of China in 1681. The princes of the Khalkhas acknowledged the Manchu emperor as their great khan in 1651. They placed themselves under the protection of Emperor K'ang-hsi (1654-1722) by swearing allegiance to him at Lake Dolonnor in eastern Chahar in what is present-day Inner Mongolia on 22 May 1691.

Galdan, *Boshoghtu Khan* of the Oirats of the Zungar state from 1671 to 1697, contested with the Manchus the control of the Khalkhas. He attacked Sayin Noyon *Tushetu Khan*, the chief prince of the Khalkhas, on 7 September 1688.

The princes of the Khalkhas neld a quriltai on the Sino-Mongolian border and petitioned *Jebtsundamba*[5] Lobzang Tenpai Gyaltshan (1635—1725), the first head of the Buddhism of Mongolia and the third son of Gombo Tushetu Khan, for advice whether to ally with China or with Russia. Although a religious leader, the Jebtsundamba wielded great political influence. Jebtsundamba Lobzang Tenpai Gyaltshan, the head of Mongolian Buddhism, and Chakhundorj Tushetu Khan, the chief prince of the Khalkhas, preferred alliance with China. They were brothers. They were not in favour of an alliance with Russia because their enemies, the Oirats, were in alliance with Russia. Their branch of the Borjgid clan was the most distinguished of the Khalkhas. The Jebtsundamba said :

> Our people have received kindness from the Emperor [of China. Now, because we wish to escape the Oirat soldiers, we wish to ally with the Tsar [Peter the Great of Russia]. The Russians have never worshipped the Buddha ; their customs are not the same as ours ; they are different in language ; and they wear different dress. Therefore, to ally with the Tsar cannot be proper policy. It is best that we all migrate to the interior and ally with the Emperor. Thus we may find prosperity for ten thousand years.

The Jebtsundamba, the Tushiyetu Khan and other princes of the Khalkhas along with their subjects migrated to the south to seek the protection of the Manchu emperor of China. Emperor K'ang-hsi confirmed Jebtsundamba Lobzang Tenpai Gyaltshan as the head of Mongolian Buddhism and conferred on him the title of *Khutukhtu*, the Living Buddha. This situation lasted till the end of Manchu rule in China in 1911. Interestingly, the eighth and the last Jebtsundamba, Lobzang Chhokyi Nyima Tenzin (1871- 924), declared the independence of the Mongols from the Manchus on 1 December 1911.

Mongolian historians have tended to be critical of the decision of the Jebtsundamba and the Khalkha princes to ally with the Manchus in return for help against the invasion of Galdan Boshoghtu Khan in 1688-91. According to them, the Jebtsundamba and the Khalkha princes should have preferred to settle with the kindred Oirats rather than ally with the alien Manchus in the overall Mongol interests. This might have avoided, they seem to be of the opinion, the complications with the Hans in 1911-21, and subsequently.

Commander Fiyanggu of the Manchu expeditionary force defeated Gandan in 1696 at Zuunmod, east of present-day Ulan Bator. Galdan escaped and died in 1697. The Khalkha refugees returned from China to the eastern part of the their native land. The Manchus integrated the Khalkhas into their empire. Of course, they were not able to pacify the Oirats until the campaign of Emperor Ch'ien Lung (1723-96) in 1755-57 against Amursana or Amursanag,

Introduction 13

who had rebelled against the Manchu emperor. Amursana was the Manchu *amban* (governor) of Uliyasutai from 1754 to 1755.

Amursana, who along with his family escaped to Siberia in Russia, died of smallpox in the environs of Tobolsk where he had sought asylum. Before his escape he had even tried to join forces with the Khalkha insurgents under Chengun *Zasaghtu Khan*. He had also requested Russia for help against the Manchu forces. Owing to the stipulations of the Chinese-Russian treaty signed at Kyakhta on 12 October 1727, which ended the alliance between the Oirats and the Russians and prevented the Russians from going into north-east Turkistan, the Russian government had declined his request. It had, however, assured him a welcome in Russia should he seek asylum. Anyway the defeat of Amursana fundamentally changed the situation in Central Asia. It completed the conquest of the Mongol land by the Manchus. Thus the Chinese-Russian treaty of 1727 actually resulted in the final Manchu victory in Zungaria and Kashgaria of East Turkistan.

The Chinese-Russian rivalry over Mongolia was quite considerable by the end of the seventeenth century. China sucessfully insulated the Russian, from the Mongols through the Chinese-Russian peace treaties signed at Nerchinsk on 27 August 1689 and at Kyakhta on 12 October 1727. The treaty of 1689, which defined the boundary between China and Russia in general terms, established the dividing line of the boundary of Manchuria, including the Barga Mongols as well as the Dagurs and Solon tribes south of the Amuro. River, at the watershed between the Amur and Lena rivers and left the Amur territories within China. The treaty of 1727, which defined the Chinese-Russian boundary of Khalkha Mongolia, also settled the question of trade between China and Russia. It set up two places for exchange of goods between them—Kyakhta and Nerchinsk. The Chinese set up border posts across the Khalkha and Transbaikal regions. Till 1858 China did not permit any Europeans, not even the Russians, to settle in Mongolia. They totally excluded the Russians from Mongolia except for their annual caravans across Mongolia to China. Russia opened its first trading post at Urga in Mongolia in 1860, although the first Russian mission of Ivan Petrov and Vasily Tyumenets to Mongolia dated to 1615-16. By 1900 the Chinese could not prevent the Russians from moving into Mongolia. And, in the event of the partition of China among the treaty powers after the defeat of the Boxer movement (the siege of foreign legations at Peking by the Boxers from 20 June to 14 August 1900), Mongolia would certainly have gone to Russia.

On the morrow of the Chinese revolution of 1911 the Mongols succeeded in throwing off the yoke of the Manchu Ch'ing dynasty of China with Russian diplomatic support. In August 1911 the Mongols sent a delegation to Tsar Nikolai II (r. 1895-1917), carrying a letter signed by the Jebtsundamba and the four chief princes of the Khalkhas, to solicit Russian assistance to save Mongolia against Chinese oppression. This letter is rather interesting in the context of the Mongol reorientation from China in the south to Russia in th north :

> The omnipotent White Tsar of the great Russian people, being powerful, strong and charitable, protests the yellow people and is himself the incarnation of virtue. If we assist one another, we will not lose our former position. According to the experience of many nations, any small people can become strong if it is supported by a great people. There is a saying that a great state helps a small state. Mighty White Tsar, consider our condition with pity and magnanimity. Humbly imploring help and protection, as do those who long for rain in times of great drought, and speaking but the truth, we present you this worthless gift.

The Mongols, like the other peoples of Central Asia, called the emperor of Russia "White Tsar".[6] It is interesting to note that, in the Mongol thinking, the concept of *Kalki Avatar* (Incarnation of the Machine Age, i.e. the Present Age) of Shambhala had become identifiable with the Tsar, and Shambhala with Russia.

Tsar Nikolai II did not receive the delegation of the Mongols. The Mongol question seems to have arisen unexpectedly. suddenly as it were. Perhaps Russian diplomacy was not ready for it. Manchuria ratner than Mongolia was the main concern of Russia's China and East Asia policy then. However, Neratov, then acting foreign minister of Russia, reported to the Tsar that the "movement that has emerged among the Mongols can be made use of in our relations with China". Owing to the political situation in the Far East/East Asia and the Near East/West Asia then, the government of the Tsar did not think it proper to take any active interest in Mongolia. None the less, it decided to increase its small military force stationed in Urga, capital of Mongolia, as the guard of the consulate and to point out to the Manchu government of China that the Tsar's government would regard Manchu measures in Mongolia as inimical to Russia. For preventing Manchu reprisals against the delegation of the

Introduction

Mongols returning from St. Petersburg, it sent a Cossack contingent with it for protection.

On 10 October 1911 the Chinese declared, in the city of Wuhan, an end to the Manchu Ch'ing dynasty. The six-year old Emperor Hsuan T'ung, better known by his later name of Henry Pu-yi, abidcated on 12 February 1912. China become a republic although Hsuan Tung kept his title and court. Abdication of the Manchu Ch'ing dynasty on 12 February 1912 also freed the Mongols of their ties with China.

The Khalkhas drove out the Manchu officials from Urga. On 1 December 1911 they declared Mongolia an independent state. The declaration said:

> Our Mongalia, when first founded, was an independent country. According to this age-old right, therefore, Mongolia declares itself an independent state that will establish a new government which will deal with the country's affairs in which no other authorities may interfere. In keeping with this decision, we Mongols declare ourselves free now on outside the jurisdiction of the Manchu or Han officials [of China]. They have lost their power. They should leave our country and return to their own at once.

On 29 December the Mongols proclaimed the Jebtsundamba as the *Bogdo Khan* (Holy Emperor) with supreme administrative authority. His choice as the Bogdo Khan by the Mongols was natural. He was well known throughout the Mongol world. He was not only the head but also the symbol of Mongolian Buddhism. The Bogdo Khan renamed Urga and called it *Liislel Khuree*, meaning Capital Monastery. The Mongols also gave their Mongolia a national flag.

The movement for independence united all the Mongols. The government of the Bogdo Khan aimed at the creation of an independent state of the entire Mongol land—*Veke Mongol Ulus* (Great Mongol State). The Mongols of Inner Mongolia favoured unification with the independent Mongolian state. The Mongols of present-day Inner Mongolian Autonomous Region (IMAR) of the People's Republic of China (PRC) thus are a national minority of China only because of historical circumstances.

The proclamation of Mongolian independence was mainly the work of religious and secular lords. Nevertheless, it created conditions for the emergence of the proletarian leadership of the Mongolian Revolution of 10 July 1921. The decade from 1911 to 1921 was indeed crucial in the history of modern Mongolia. Chinese historians look upon the proclamation of Mongolian independence as an event precipitated by the policy of Russia to extend its border up to the Great Wall of China.

On the morrow of the declaration of Mongolia as an independent state, a Russian scholar[7] formulated the Russian ambitions thus :

> In its own interests, commercial and military, Russia must deprive China of any opportunity to move close to our borders and to establish itself there. This can be done by consolidating the independence of Mongolia from China. Along with a move so uniquely advantageous to us the question invariably arises. Is Mongolia able to maintain its own independence? The only answer is : No. China is too big and Mongolia is too small, and helpless. Both by open force and economic tactics China can destroy the recently constituted state of the nomads. There is no other solution to the problem of the Mongols, but the fulfilment of their fervent hopes for the association of Mongolia with Russia for ever. Therewith we shall achieve every possible thing. We shall rescue the Mongols from a sure destruction under the pressure of China; we shall find faithful subjects in the acquired people, fit for military service, and loving us, who will become our combat vanguards; we shall fulfil our historical tasks of uniting Mongolia whose millions are already distributed among us; we shall have a rich region with fertile land, which is also suitable for our settlers; we shall obtain an extensive market for selling our goods and produce; we shall open a source abundant with raw materials not only for Siberia, but for European Russia as well; we shall draw nearer to China and facilitate the sale of our own products there, we shall seize a wide, impassable belt in the desert in central Mongolia which will firmly guarantee us from invasion from Asia. All these are immeasurable advantages.

Russia first recognized the autonomy of Mongolia by signing with the Mongols an agreement attaching a commercial protocol, in Urga on 3 November 1912. Although the agreement was not one the Mongols had desired, they endorsed it as the Bogdo Khan government wanted to use it to prove that it had been recognized as an independent state. The Chinese repudiated the Russo-Mongol agreement. Thus Chinese-Russian discussions concerning the status of

Mongolia began in 1912 for the first time. A Chinese-Russian declaration concluded in Peking on 5 November 1913 developed the principle of autonomous Mongolia under the suzerainty of China. The Bogdo Khan regime vigorously refused to accept the Chinese-Russian declaration although it was a mere statement of principle, binding neither contracting party.

Eventually China, Mongolia and Russia concluded a treaty at the end of a tripartite conference (1914-15) held on the basis of the Russo-Mongol agreement of 1912 and the Russo-Chinese declaration of 1913 and signed at Kyakhta on 7 July 1915. This treaty split Mongolia into two parts—Inner Mongolia and Outer Mongolia. It made Inner Mongolia, adjoining China, a part of China and Outer Mongolia, remote from China, an autonomous state under the suzerainty of China. Yuan Shi-kai (1859-1916), presedent of the Republic of China from 1912 to 1916, also applied this principle in his negotiations with the British in connection with the question of Tibet. He really did well, for China's diplomatic position was quite weak then. It is interesting to note that, up to this point, Russian policy towards Mongolia and British policy towards Tibet were quite alike. The maintenance of China's political connection with Mongolia and Tibet was in both Russian and British interests there.

The tripartite Chinese-Mongolian-Russian treaty also granted amnesty for the Barguts and Inner Mongols who had fled to Urga after the declaration of the independence of Mongolia.

The delegation of China at the Kyakhta conference, it appears, also tried to make Outer Mongolia a part of China, but the skilful diplomacy of the delegation of Russia frustrated the designs of the delegaiion of China. Russia was equally responsible for blocking the fulfilment of the aspirations of the Mongols. It supported the concept of the autonomy of Mongolia under the suzerainty of China (as a sop to Chinese feeling), but it did not support the concept of a pan-Mongolia. Perhaps the Russo-Japanese agreements defining the Russian and Japanese interests in Manchuria and Mongolia, which, particularly the convention of 1912, included Outer Mongolia in the Russian sphere, constrained it from doing so.[8] Also, these treaties formed the very bases of Russian policy in the Far East/ East Asia. How interesting if Mongolia had to be subordinated to Japan's interests in the region. Perhaps Russia had its eyes on Uryanghai, Western Mongolia. Buryatia had already become part of Russia by the end of the seventeenth century.

Anyhow the separation of Outer Mongolia from China and the establishment of a Russian protectorate over it clearly had been the goals of Russian policy since 1911. But, since Russia had not wanted to irritate China, it created the fiction of China's suzerainty over it. Thus the Mongol attempt to include the entire Mongol land, particularly Barga, Inner Mongolia and Uryanghai, in the autonomous state of Mongolia in 1911-15 failed.The government of autonomous Mongolia had even militarily supported the movement and given asylum to many leaders of the movement for the independence of Mongolia such as Toghtokh and Utai. The Inner Mongols had also played an important role in the movement for the independence of Outer Mongolia. However, because of Chinese economic and security considerations, the Mongols of Inner Mongolia were never able to separate from China and join Outer Mongolia.

The Altai and Uryanghai regions were not involved in the struggle for the independence of Mongolia. Russia preferred the Altai mountain range as the western boundary of autonomous Mongolia. The Manchus had administered the Altai and Uryanghai districts from Kobdo in western Mongolia. China had not completely absorbed the Altai district in the Sinkiang province before 1919. So long as Mongolia was part of China, Uryanghai was part of Mongolia under the amban of Kobdo. The Kyakhta treaty of 1727 was not very clear in defining the border line between China and Russia in the vicinity of Uryanghai. The boundary commission, which drew up the line, assumed the Sayan Mountain range north of Uryanghai as identical with the Tannu Ola range in the south. The Chinese-Russian border protocol signed in Chuguchak/Tarbagatai on 25 September 1864, which defined the dividing line between the Chinese and Russian empires, recognized Uryanghai as part of Mongolia/China.

Thus, in 1911, the Mongols considered Uryanghai as legitimately falling within the Mongol land. Autonomous Mongolia claimed jurisdiction over Uryanghai. The people of Uryanghai claimed Mongol culture as their heritage. They desired to become part of the Mongol nation. Anyway the tsar's government formulated a policy against the unification of Uryanghai with Mongolia. Russia detached Uryanghai in 1911 and made it a protectorate on 11 April 1914. It had to recognize large and well-known Mongolia; it annexed small and obscure Ureanghai without any qualm. The Russians had also intended to make Barga in northwest Manchuria, bordering Outer Mongolia and Russia, a part of their Siberia. This is really why the tsar's government did not agree to the inclusion of all Mongol lands with autonomous Mongolia.

The government of autonomous Mongolia sought to enter into diplomatic relations with a number of countries such as Japan, Germany, France, Britain, America and others. To its disappointment, except Russia, no country recognized it.

The government of revolutionary Russia declared to the government and people of Mongolia on 3 August 1919 :

> The Russian people have renounced all treaties with the Japanese and Chinese governments in regard to Mongolia. Mongolia is a free country. The Russian counsellors, consuls, bankers and the rich who had been having the Mongols well in their hands by using force and gold should be expelled from Mongolia. The entire power and justice should belong to the Mongols. No foreigner has the right to interfere in the internal affairs of Mongolia. With the 1915 agreement repealed Mongolia as an independent country has the right to communicate directly with all other nations without the guardianship of either Peking or Petrogard.

Perhaps the Republic of China did not understand the meaning of the Marxist language of this declaration. It cancelled the autonomy of Outer Mongolia by a decree on 22 November 1919. It also abolished the post of its high commissioner for the pacification of Outer Mongolia and the northwest frontier of China on 8 September 1920. A Chinese military force under General Hsu Shu-ts'ang, "Little Hsu," occupied Urga. It forced the Bogdo Khan government to request China to abolish Mongolian autonomy. It dismantled the Mongolian national government and demobilized the Mongolian national army and seized its munitions. The Chinese militarists patronized the feudal lay princes and nobles and harassed the nationalist lamas and laymen of Mongolia. According to Chiang Kai-shek (1886-1975),[9] the Mongols gave up their independence and came back into China's fold as a result of the Soviet revolution. The Mongols and the Russians, revolutionaries and non-revolutionaries, have not responded to this. Revolutionary Russia was not yet strong enough to prevent this. Of course, its envoys in Urga and Peking demanded maintenance of their rights in Mongolia, although to no avail.

Mongolian historians have been rather severe in their judgement of the lay and monastic leaders, civil servants and intellectuals who voted for the abolition of Mongolian autonomy. The then political situation in Mongolia and its neighbouring region was most difficult, the Mongols had no alternative or option. Significantly, however, the Bogdo Khan, though seriously ill, neither agreed to the abolition of Mongolian autonomy nor signed the petition for its abolition.

Early in October 1920 the Russian White Guards, who had been thrown out of Russia by the Revolution of 1917, entered Mongolia under Ungern-Sternberg, who had joined the young Cossack officer Ataman Grigorii Semenov. Ataman Semenov had mustered Cossacks, Mongols and adventurers to fight the troops of revolutionary Russia. On 17 November the Chinese garrison repulsed Ungern. However, in February 1921, Ungern entered Urga, proclaimed the independence of Mongolia from China and restored the Bogdo Khan as the supreme ruler of the entire Mongol land.

This created a crisis, and complications for revolutionary Russia. A military force of the Red Army with support from the Mongolian people but to the annoyance of a helpless China crossed the border into Mongolia in pursuit of Ungern's White Guards in June 1921. On 21 June a Soviet statement said: "The armies of Workers' and Peasants' Russia and the Far Eastern Rapublic will not remain any longer in Mongolia than will be necessary to defeat the common enemy: the tsarist general, the bloody Ungern . . ."

A joint Mongolian-Soviet force of 10,000 troops descended on Urga on 6 July. On 10 July, with the help of Soviet troops, the Mongolian People's Party (later the Mongolian People's Revolutionary Party), a nationalist party founded and led by Damdingiin Sukhe Bator (1893-1923), ended Chinese occupation of Mongolia and proclaimed the Mongolian national government, installing the Bogdo Khan as a monarch. The Mongolian revolutionists expected the Bogdo Khan leadership to give their regime legltimacy and ensure popular support. On 12 July the Mongolian national government requested Soviet troops to stay on in Mongolia. These troops captured Ungern on 22 July 1921 and executed him on 15 November. They remained in Mongolia until 1925.

Under the Oath-taking Treaty of 1 November 1921 the Bogdo Khan became the first head of state, and Bodoo the first prlme minister of the government of revolutionary Mongolia.

China's inability to control the activities of the White Guards served as the justification for the alignment of the Mongolian People's Army with the Red Army of Soviet Russia, then engaged in a civil war in Siberia. This does not mean that the Red Army of Soviet Russia was behind the Mongolian revolution of 1921, although the Russian revolution of 1917 had directly influenced it. The roots of the Mongol revolution lay deep in Mongol history and in the conditions of Mongol society. Soviet support only helped to make Mongolia independent. Anyway the Mongol revolution is a watershed in the history of modern Mongolia. It ended China's hold on Mongolia and opened up new prospects for the Mongols.

With the entry of Soviet troops into Mongolia revived the struggle over its status between China and Russia. This struggle perhaps is not yet over. Or is it?

The history of relations between China, Mongolia and Russia in modern times suggests that Mongolia was not a dependency of China or of Russia. Mongolia had been an irritant to both China and Russia since 1691. The Chinese and Russian manoeuvres over Mongolia during the closing years of the Tsarist period and the opening years of the Soviet period in Russia are particularly significant in this connection. The Russians supported the principle of the autonomy of Mongolia because of its importance, especially under their protection, to Siberia's military security. Initially the Soviets seem to have supported Mongolia for the same reason. Later, there was a significant change in the Soviet policy towards Mongolia.

Thus Afghanistan and Mongolia, which had succumbed to the shackles of imperialism, had shaken off the imperialist hold by the early 1920s. Both Britain and Russia accepted the independent status of Afghanistan. In the case of Mongolia, only Russia recognized its independence. Afghanistan's relations with Germany during the world war of 1914-1918 were as much a consequence of its distrust of British intentions towards it as those of Russia. Mongolia's relations with Japan during 1919-1921 were as much a consequence of its distrust of Chinese intentions towards it as those of Russia.

Owing to their location, both Afghanistan and Mongolia have a long history of strategic importance. Afghanistan and Russia became adjacent countries only in the 1860s and have been close neighbours since the 1920s. The USSR has been dominating Afghanistan since the end of the 1970s. For over two hundred years Russia tried to extend its influence to Mongolia. Mongolia and the USSR became close neighbours in the 1920s. The USSR has been dominating Mongolia since then. Hence the framework of this study *Afghanistan, Mongolia and USSR*: the political connection of Afghanistan and Mongolia with the USSR from the 1920s to the present day.

NOTES AND REFERENCES

1. *Sardar*, a military title.
2. Persia's name officially changed to Iran in 1935.
3. A son of Amir Dost Muhammad. He was Amir of Afghanistan from 1866 to 1867.
4. First weekly newspaper of Afghanistan.
5. *Jebtsundamba*, a title of the Buddhism of Tibet. The Dalai Lama V, the Great conferred this title on the first head of Mongolian Buddhism, known as Bogdo Gegen (Holy Teaeher) to the Mongols, in 1650.
6. Ivan IV the Terrible was the first emperor of Russia to assume the title *Belyi Tsar*, "White Tsar", for use in his correspondence with the peoples of the steppe. The term had nothing to do with his race. It merely reproduced the Mongol—Turkic, associations of points on the compass with a set of colours. In this sense, the Belyi Tsar meant only the ruler of the east. The later Tsars of Russia used this title in their dealings with the peoples of the east. Thus it became the common title of the Tsars of Russia among the peoples of the east. Old Russian sources knew the eastern peoples, who joined Batu Khan's banners in the thirteenth century, as Tatars.
7. V. Tomolin, *Mongolia and its Contemporary Importance to Russia* (In Russian), Moscow, 1913.
8. The Russo-Japanese peace treaty, signed at portsmouth (New Hampshire, USA) in 1905, concerned Russian territorial concestion in southern Manchuria to Japan. After the overthrow of the Manchu, Ch'sing dynasty in China, Manchuria became a virtual Japanese province under the Chinese warlord Chang Tso-lin
9. *China's Destiny* (in Chinese), Chunking, 1943; rev.. 1944: English ed: New York, 1947, p 52.

2

AFGHANISTAN, 1919—1945

The Russian Soviet Federated Socialist Rupublic (RSFSR)[1] recongnized the independence of Afghanistan on 27 March 1919. It was the first country to do so. The Soviet government also informed Amir Amanullah (1892-1929) that it had annulled the Tsarist treaties and agreements infringing upon sovereignty particularly the Anglo-Russian convention of 31 August 1907.

Amir Amanullah wrote the leaders of revolutionary Russia with the desire to establish diplomatic relations. In his letter to Mikhail Ivonovich Kalinin (1875-1946), Chairman of the RSFSR Central Executive Committee (later the Supreme Soviet) on 7 April 1919, he said:

> Afghanistan, by its very spirit and nature, has since its emergence as an independent country been the champion of freedom and equality, However, for certain reasons it has up till now been unable to establish relations with other countries and peoples.
> Since you, Your Excellency, my great and gracious friend, President of the Great Russian State, along with your comrades, who are friends of humanity, have undertaken the honourable and noble task of concern for the peace and good of people and have declared the principle of freedom and equality of the countries and nations of the whole world, I am happy to send to you this friendly message for the first time from independent and free Afghanistan on behalf of the Afghan people striving for progress.

Afghanistan and the RSFSR then concluded their first treaty, initialled in Kabul on 13 September 1920 and signed in Moscow on 28 February 1921. Each contracting party recognized the independnce of the other. It was the first equal treaty that Afghanistan signed with any country. After the signing of the Afghan-Soviet treaty of 1921 Vladimir Ilyich Lenin (1870-1924), Chairman of the Council of the

People's Commissars (renamed Council of Ministers in March 1946), sent a friendly reply to Amanullah on 27 May 1919:

> The Russian Soviet Government and the High Afghan State have common interests in the East. Both states cherish their independence and want independence and freedom for themselves and for all the peoples of the East. Friendship between them is not only because of this, but more because of the fact that there are no problems between Afghanistan and Russia which can cause disagreements or even cast a shadow on Russo-Afghan friendship. The old imperialist Russia has disappeared forever, and the High Afghan State now has for its northern neighbour the new Soviet Russia that has extended a hand of friendship to all the peoples of the East and to the Afghan people in the first place. Convinced that the bonds of friendship between Russia and Afghanistan will continue to strengthen, I take the liberty of expressing to you my sympathy and confidence that no one, either by force or cunning, will undermine the independence of the High Afghan State.[2]

Was not Lenin initiating, in this message to Amanullah, the popular style of Soviet diplomacy, that is, to make promises which might never be fulfilled and agree upon principles which might never be kept in practice?

Georgi Vasilyevich Chicherin (1872—1936)[3] thus elaborated the basic point of Lenin's policy towards Afghanistan in his instructions to the Soviet Plenipotentiary Yakov Surits in Afghanistan on 3 June 1921:

> Our policy in the East is not aggressive; it is a policy of peace and friendship. Throughout your work you must systematically stress this basic point. The main object of your work in Kabul is to promote our friendship with Afghanistan. Friendship presupposes reciprocal assistance. In line with our desire to facilitate the development and promote the prosperity of the friendly Afghan state as far as possible, we are prepared to give it our utmost assistance. You must study the needs and requirements of Afghanistan and elucidate to us the wishes of its Government so that in carrying out and fulfilling the Russo-Afghan treaty we may give it all the assistance we can with the object of facilitating its development and promoting its prosperity.
>
> You are instructed to pay particularly close attention to the

Amir's programme of reform. At Afghanistan's present stage of development, an enlightened absolutism of the type that we had in our country in the eighteenth century is of great progressive significance; we cannot and must not approach Afghanistan with the yardstick of the economically developed countries. Naturally, we must neither forget for a minute nor leave in the shade the tremendous distinction between the programme of Communism and the programme that is being fulfilled and can be fulfilled by the present Afghan Government. We must not for a minute conceal our stand. But this need not prevent us from expressing sympathy with and rendering our utmost assistance to the reformist undertakings of the friendly Afghan Government and to the progressive creative work of the enlightened absolutism in Afghanistan. We do not for a moment become either monarchists or adherents of absolutism. This must be made clear to everybody. Yet we render all the assistance we can to the reformist undertakings of the progressive minded Amir.

You must avoid altogether the fatal mistake of trying to impose Communism on that country. We say to the Afghan Government: you have one political system and we have another; but we are linked up by our community of aspirations for complete sovereignty and independence. We do not interfere in your internal affairs; we do not intrude upon the activity of your people. We do not for a moment contemplate imposing on your people a programme that is alien to them at the present stage of their development.

The Soviet Government also agreed to return to Afghanistan territory in the Panjdeh district and to pay Afghanistan a yearly subsidy of 1,000,000 gold or silver rubles, which the British had formerly paid to Afghanistan but which they had stopped paying after the Anglo-Afghan War of 1919.

The 1921 Afghan Soviet treaty also recognized Bukhara and Khiva as independent countries. Amanullah established diplomatic relations with Bukhara and Khiva. When the Soviet Government annexed Bukhara and Khiva to the RSFSR, the Basmachi nationalists fled to the Pamir mountains and Afghanistan and continued to raid Soviet territory from there. Said Mir Alim, Amir of Bukhara, escaped to Afghanistan on 5 March 1921.

Amanullah's government protested against the entry of Soviet troops into Bukhara. The reply of Fyodor Pyodorovich Raskolnikov first Soviet Ambassador to Afghanistan, on 20 February 1922 reveals a pattern, and bears quoting:

> Concerning the question of the independence of Bukhara and Khiva, this has been provided for in the treaty agreed to and signed by the two Governments of Russia and Afghanistan. The Government which I represent has always recognized and respected the independence of the two Governments of Bukhara and Khiva. The presence of a limited contingent of troops belonging to my Government is due to temporary requirements expressed and made known to us by the Government of Bukhara. This arrangement has been agreed to with the provision that whenever the Government of Bukhara so requests, not a single Russian soldier will remain on the soil of Bukhara. The extension of our friendly assistance in no way constitutes an interference against the independence of the sovereign state of Bukhara. If the Government of Bukhara should cease to formulate its request and should have been dissatisfied with the continuation of such brotherly assistance, then the Government I represent shall most immediately withdraw its troops

Amanullah conferred upon Raskolnikov the title "Sardar", the highest in Afghanistan, for the good work he did in the cause of Soviet-Afghan friendship. Raskolnikov probably never used the title nor wore the decoration.

In 1923 Amanullah appointed Abdul Hadi Dawi, associate of Mahmud Tarzi, as head of the fact-finding mission, with the rank of ambassador plenipotentiary, concerning the independence of Bukhara. Dawi was then adviser in the Ministry of Foreign Affairs (Kabul). The Amir also supported the anti-Soviet Basmachi nationalist movement in Central Asia.

On a number of occasions, Soviet troops chased the Basmachis into Afghanistan. In 1925 they took by force Urta Tagai, an island in the Amu Darya, and evicted the Afghan garrison from Yangi Qala. Kabul lodged a strong protest. A joint Afghan-Soviet commission investigated the dispute and found that the island belonged to Afghanistan. The Union of Soviet Socialist Republics (USSR)[4] recognized the economic importance of the island to Afghanistan. The commission concluded a protocol to this effect in Kabul on 15 August 1926.

The origin of the dispute could be traced back to the first definition of the Afghan-Russian frontier in the 1880s. In the first decade of the present century, the Amu Darya changed its course, moving north. The Afghans moved into the area that emerged following the river changing its course, and the government of Afghanistan administered it. None the less, the government of Russia continued to claim the area south of the river. Hence the dispute as to who actually owned it.

The protocol of 1926 encouraged the two governments to promote relations between the two countries, which concluded their first treaty of neutrality and non-aggression in Paghman (Afghanistan) on 31 August 1926. This treaty stipulated non-interference by either country in the other's affairs. By it the two governments pledged against the use of their territories as a base for any subversive activity aimed against each other. Amanullah specially pledged against the use of Afghan territory as a base for any subversive activity aimed against the Soviet Union.

To establish diplomatic contacts with the outside world, King Amanullah undertook extensive tours of Asian and European countries, including Britain and the USSR, in 1928. Besides adroitly handling the most difficult situations in his relations with Britain and the USSR, he established Afghanistan among the nations of the world by securing their recognition.

Amanullah dropped the title *Amir* and assumed the title *Shah* (King), with the dignity of His Majesty in 1926. He was a monarch with a modern outlook. Quite early in his reign, on 9 April 1923, he proclaimed the first constitution of the country. He also built a palace of his dreams and named it *Darulaman* (abode of peace). As part of his programme of the madernization of the education system, he established three schools—the Lycee Istaqlal, modelled on the French system, for girls of the *elite* families of Kabul under a French headmistress in 1923; the Amani (later Nizat) High School, on the German model and staffed by German as well as Afghan teachers in 1924; and the Ghazi with English as the medium of instruction in 1927. He sent a few Afghans to Europe also to get modern education and a group of girls to Turkey to train as nurses. Under conservative pressure he suppressed girls schools in the country in 1924. His efforts to set up modern institutions in Afghanistan ultimately cost him his throne.

After the flight of Amanullah from Kabul early in 1929, General Mohammed Nadir Khan (1883-1933), son of Sardar Yusuf Khan and cousin of Amanullah, returned from France and fought decisive battles with the Bacha-i-Sakka. Nadir Khan had been one of

Amanullah's generals, but, owing to differences with the latter, he had gone into voluntary exile in France in 1924. After becoming king of Afghanistan on 16 October 1929, Nadir Khan pronounced a sentence of death on the Bacha-i-Sakka.

King Nadir Shah pledged to follow in the footsteps of King Amanullah. But he adopted methods different from those of Amanullah. He proclaimed a constitution for Afghanistan in October 1931. This provided for hereditary monarchy, establishing the kingship of Afghanistan in the family of King Nadir Shah. It recognized the *Loya Jirga* (Great Assembly) of the chiefs and elders of the tribes of Afghanistan as the highest repository of power in the land and gave them a share in the governance of Afghanistan.

The constitution of 1931 vested the executive, judicial and legislative powers in the king. Under the constitution, the king appointed the prime minister, who, in his turn, chose his own council of ministers with the approval of the king. Nadir Shah appointed his elder brother Sardar Hashim Khan as his *Wazir-i-Azam* (prime minister.) He also appointed his younger brothers to high offices of state. The constitution gave the king control over the armed forces and royal expenditure. Further, the authority to declare war, make peace and extend clemency also vested with the king.

Nadir Shah declared primary education free and compulsory for all children. He established a medical college in 1932. He encouraged Afghan students to go abroad for study and training. To promote national and tribal harmony, he introduced several important measures. For example, he ordered the repair of the grave of Emperor Zahiruddin Babar (1483-1530), founder of the Mughal Empire, in the Bag-i-Babar. Indeed, he was a shrewd ruler.

Nadir Shah tried to pursue a policy of balance between Britain and the Soviet Union. He also broadened the diplomatic infrastructure of Afghanistan. On 18 November 1930 Afghanistan concluded a treaty with Japan in London. Afghanistan and Japan exchanged legation-level diplomats. The Japan connection was useful to Afghanistan. Japan's emergence as a military and commercial power in the 1920s made a deep impression on Afghanistan. Japanese commercial interests in Afghanistan also influenced the Afghan strategy of persuading its neighbours, Britain and the Soviet Union, that they could no longer dictate terms.

In the 1930s, Japanese engineers made surveys of the Helmand River basin for the purpose of digging a canal for irrigating the Girishk region, west of Kandahar. However, the world war (1939-

45) interrupted the Japanese project. After the war, in 1946, the government of Afghanistan engaged the Morrison-Knudsen Company (of Boise, Idaho, USA) to complete the Helmand reclamation and irrigation project. Later, in the mid-1950s, Afghanistan partly accepted official US aid for the purpose. US involvement in the Helmand water and land development project lasted three decades. The post-1978 revolution complications marked the end of the project.

According to the Afghans, extraneous considerations were responsible for the US interest in the development of the Helmand Valley. The Afghans felt that a permanent settlement there of the Kuchi nomads, used to annual winter migrations across the Durand Line was of greater advantage to Pakistan than to Afghanistan itself.

King Nadir renegotiated the Afghan-Soviet treaty of 31 August 1926 in Kabul on 24 June 1931. Among other accords, Afghanistan and the Soviet Union concluded, in September 1932, an agreement for the appointment of commissioners to study frontier questions.

Sardar Mohammed Zahir Khan was barely twenty years old when he succeeded his father King Nadir upon the latter's assassination in Kabul on 8 November 1933. He kept his uncle Sardar Hashim Khan as his prime minister. He also kept his other uncles Shah Mahmud and Shah Wali in the high offices of state.

King Zahir Shah sought to maintain correct relations with both Britain and the Soviet Union and close relations with Iran, Turkey and other Muslim countries. He also sought to promote other international relations. He secured Afghanistan's admission into the League of Nations under the sponsorship of Turkey on 17 November 1934.

The governments of Afghanistan and the United States of America (USA) concluded a provisional agreement, the first agreement between the two countries, in Paris on 26 March 1936. President Franklin D. Roosevelt had recognized Afghanistan in a letter to King Zahir Shah on 21 August 1934. The Afghan-US agreement contained clauses on diplomatic representation. The US government accredited its minister to Iran simultaneously to Afghanistan. On 6 July 1942 the United States established legation-level diplomatic relations with Afghanistan. The US legation in Kabul was particularly useful during the world war of 1939-1945 in arranging land-lease supplies to China through the Pamir route.

The government of King Zahir Shah concluded a protocol to the Afghan-Soviet treaty of 1931 in Moscow on 29 March 1936.

Moscow discouraged Kabul from taking an active interest in the Islamic Republic of Eastern Turkistan (IRET) established in 1933. In the Soviet view, the Islamaic Republic of Eastern Turkistan was an anti-Soviet Anglo-Japanese creation. The Soviets helped the Chinese to annihilate the IRET. The Soviet Government also did not approve of Afghanistan's association with the treaty of 8 July 1937, commonly known as the Saadabad Pact on account of its having been signed at Saadabad Palace near Tehran. The Saadabad Pact, which allied Afghanistan with Iran, Iraq and Turkey, aroused Soviet fear of increasing Turkish influence in Afghanistan. For Turkey, though not hostile to the Soviet Union, was supporting the camp headed by Britain. The preliminary talks for the Saadabad Pact had been held in Moscow in 1934.

During the mid-1930s, Afghanistan developed friendly relations with Germany and concluded several economic and other agreements with that country. Under the protocol signed by Afghanistan and Germany in October 1936 Germany promised to deliver arms to Afghanistan. What is interesting is how it could do so. For the Afghan-Soviet treaty of 1931, forbade Afghanistan and the Soviet Union from entering into an alliance with third countries that might threaten either Afghan or Soviet interests. However, Germany became the third power in Afghanistan. A weekly air service, inaugurated in 1937, linked Berlin with Kabul.

Afghanistan and China are old neighbours. Chinese rule, however nominal, extended up to Afghanistan as early as the first century A.D. Buddhism spread to Changan and Loyang in China from Afghanistan, a part of India then, and Indo-Iranian kingdoms along the great trade centres and routes in the first and second centuries A.D. The first Chinese pilgrims travelled to Afghanistan and India in the third and fourth centuries A.D. This traffic between Afghanistan and China continued until the end of the Buddhist/Hindu period, and the Islamization of Afghanistan, in the first half of the eleventh century.

There was no effective connection between Afghanistan and China in medieval times except the Mongol hold of both. The Manchu Emperor Ch'ien Lung (1711-96) threatened to attack Samarkand in 1762. Ahmad Shah despatched a force against the Manchu expedition in response to an appeal from the chiefs of the Kazak tribes and the Khan of Kokand. Difficulties between Afghanistan and China continued (on the Balkh side) during the time of Timur Shah, son and successor of Ahmad Shah. The decline of the fighting power of the Afghans and the emergence of the power of the English East India Company in India in the early nineteenth century led to a weakening of Afghanistan. China became weak in the latter half of the nineteenth century with no effective policy towards its neighbours, including Afghanistan. The expansion of the Western Powers into China after the T'aip'ing,[5] "Great Peace", rebellion of 1851-64 and the emergence of Russia in Central Asia in the 1860s worked as barriers against Manchu adventurism in Afghanistan.

The governments of the kingdom of Afghanistan and the Republic of China began negotiating with a view to a treaty in the 1920s. They concluded a treaty providing for exchange of diplomatic missions in Ankara on 2 March 1944.

Afghanistan remained neutral during the World War of 1939-1945. While inaugurating the Loya Jirga on 17 August 1940, Zahir Shah said that Afghanistan had observed a policy of strict neutrality since the outbreak of the European war in 1939. Both Britain and the Soviet Union pressured Afghanistan to terminate ties with Germany and Italy and to intern and expel all non-diplomatic Germans, Italians and Japanese from the country. However, King Zahir, who had looked primarily to Germany for industrial and technical assistance, maintained friendly relations with Germany even after the German attack on the Soviet Union on 22 June 1941. Equally his government allowed the Allied Powers to send war supplies to China and the Soviet Union through Afghanistan.

The Conference of the Three Great Powers, officially called the Crimean Conference and held in the Livadia Palace at Yalta (USSR) on 10 February 1945, assigned Afghanistan to the Soviet sphere of influence.

Afghanistan was one of the fifty states that founded the United Nations (UN) in San Francisco on 25 April 1945. Besides the Arab League states of Egypt, Iraq, Lebanon, Saudi Arabia and Syria, it was one of the three original world Muslim states (the other two being Iran and Turkey) signatory of the UN Charter. It joined the United Nations on 19 November 1946.

When the British withdrew from India in the summer of 1947, the *raison d'etre* for Afghanistan as a buffer between the Soviet Union and the West disappeared. This change in the political situation in the region had a profound impact on the outlook of the Afghans, especially on the policy of Afghanistan towards the Soviet Union. The United States was not yet on the horizon to enable Afghanistan to maintain a policy of balance between the north and the south.

NOTES AND REFERENCES

1. Russia's name officially changed to RSFSR in July 1918.
2. *Soviet Foreign Policy Documents*, Vol. II, Moscow, 1958, p 175.
3. People's Commissar for Foreign Affairs of RSFSR/USSR from 1918 to 1930.
4. Established in January 1923.
5. The T'aiping rebellion was a revolution against the Manchu Ching dynasty by Hund Hsu-ch' usan, a Christian mystic. British military intervention finally defeated this uprising.

3

AFGHANISTAN 1945—

The Yalta dispensation concerning the World War, which assigned Afghanistan to the Soviet sphere of influence, and the British withdrawal from India, which created a power in the region gap, was rather opportune for the Soviets to develop special relation with the Afghan. The Afghans, who were sensitively aware of all this, sought Soviet adjustments in their relations with the necessary son its King Zahir Shah initiated significant measures to meet the new circumstance, the new situation in the international life of his kingdom. The redoubtable Prime Minister, Sardar Hashim Khan, resigned on grounds of health. And his liberal younger brother, Sardar Shah Mahmud Khan, succeeded him.

On 29 March 1946, Afghanistan and the USSR renewed their treaty of neutrality and non-aggression of 1931. On 13 June 1946 they signed a protocol concerning the fixing of their boundary along the Amu and Panja rivers on the principle of *thalweg* (main channel) of these rivers and centre of the actual main channel "where thalweg is not determinable".[1] The Soviet Union recognized the economic importance of the islands in the Amu Darya to Afghanistan and settled the issue of the disputed title over them in its favour. Before the signing of this protocol, the Afghans were apprehensive that they might be asked to cede the islands to the Soviets. Thus, like the protocol of 1926, the protocol of 1946 created conditions for Moscow to come close to Kabul. Afghanistan and the Soviet Union signed an agreement on 17 July 1950 for the exchange of the agricultural produce of Afghanistan for Soviet petroleum and other commodities. The agreement specifically provided for duty—free transit of Afghan goods across Soviet territory.

The United States, which had taken Britain's place in the region, looked upon Afghanistan as one of the states of the "northern tier" defence belt, which it began building along the southern flank of the Soviet Union from Turkey to Afghanistan to contain Communism. It did fill the power gap in the region after the British withdrawal from India, but it did not offer military aid to Afghanistan to defend its independence and security. It was, therefore, unable to persuade Afghanistan to join what later became CENTO (Central Treaty Organization). Washington now maintains that it was then the US policy not to seek to engage Afghanistan as a part of the defence belt. Anyway, under the Afghanistan-United States Technical Cooperation Programme Agreement of 30 June 1953 extended by exchange of notes in Kabul on 12 October 1965, Washington gave considerable economic aid to Kabul especially in the development of the Afghan civil aviation, surface transportation, the Afghan educational system and the Helmand Valley.

Sardar Mohammed Daoud Khan (1908-78)[2], a first cousin and brother-in-law of King Zahir Shah, who became Prime Minister and Minister of the Interior and Defence on 20 September 1953, emphasized the importance of the policy of *betarafi* (neutralism) for Afghanistan. Said Daoud :

Our whole life, our whole existence revolves around one single focal point—freedom. Should we ever get the feeling that our freedom is in the slightest danger, from whatever quarter, then we should prefer to live on dry bread, or even starve, sooner than accept help that would restrict our freedom.

Only a policy of *betarafi* could enable the government of Afghanistan to balance the influence of the Soviet Union and the United States in Afghanistan. Establishing a meaningful relationship with the United States in entailed relinquishing of the relationship with the Soviet Union was also not an easy task.

At that time, the US government leaders were condemning neutralism as immoral. As the US sponsored military alliance had the distinction of being anti-Soviet, Afghanistan did not join this security system. The insistence of John Foster Dulles, the then US Secretary of State, that all states should define their position between the United States and the Soviet upon, "stand up and be counted", certainly prevented Washington from developing normal relations with the new states in Africa and Asia then. Dulles did not see the relevance of non-alignment, the middle way, in inter national relations.

N.S. Khrushchev, First (later General) Secretary of the Communist Party of the Soviet Union, and N.A. Bulganin, Chairman of the Council of Ministers of the Soviet Union, visited Afghanistan from

15 to 18 December 1955. They were the first world leaders ever to do so. In view of Daoud's attitude towards military pacts, Bulganin commended Afghanistan's "unswerving adherence to a policy of neutrality". The joint communique issued on 18 December 1955 said that the Afghan and Soviet governments based their relations on the five principles of peaceful co-existance adopted by the Afro-Asian Conference held in Bandung (Indonesia) in April 1955.

The joint communique issued at the end of King Zahir Shah's visit to the Soviet Union in September 1971 acknowledged Afghanistan's non-aligned status thus :

The Soviet side highly assesses the policy of non-alignment consistently pursued by Afghanistan and considers it an important factor in the struggle of the peoples for their freedom and independence, for strengthening peace and security, for maintaining peace and cooperation with all the peoples.

When the government of Afghanistan launched its first five year development plan (1956-62), the Soviet Union agreed to help Afghanistan. In fact, Afghanistan became the first non-communist country to receive Soviet economic aid. It seems—there is no evidence —that, because of the geographical proximity as well as political and economic backwardness of Afghanistan, the Soviet Union hoped that Afghanistan would ultimately fall into the category of countries like Mongolia and become another Soviet ally in Asia.

Whereas the United States had declined Daoud's request for aid for the modernization of the Afghan armed forces, the Soviet Union edacced to Kabul sent its army officers to the Soviet Union for training Moscow sent military supplies and advisers to Afghanistan.

Important developments on the border of Afghanistan with Pakistan such as the border closure as well as the port facilities via Krachi also led Kabul to turn to Moscow for trade transit facilities. This ultimately led to the heavy orientation of Afghanistan's trade towards the USSR and CMEA (Council on Mutual Economic Assistance) bloc countries. This proved to be rather useful to Afghanistan, because it enabled Afghanistan to meet its requirements without the expenditure of foreign exchange and without the formality of joining the Soviet Union was on the basis of barter.

Soviet aid to Afghanistan was certainly a matter of concern to the West. Western leaders felt that Soviet aid might expose Afghanistan to Communism. In addition to US aid to Afghanistan, especially in the development of the Helmand Valley and civil aviation, President D. Eisenhower visited Kabul on 8 December 1959 to express concern over Soviet aid to Afghanistan. The state visit of King Zahir and Queen Homaira to the United States on 4-16 September 1963 improved relations and understanding between Afghanistan and the United States.

As Prime Minister of Afghanistan, Daoud, who was one of the first group of students sent by King Amanullah to Europe for education and training, assumed, as it were, King Amanullah's mantle, in that he gave all his energies to promote the modernization of Afghanistan. He restored the name of the Nizat High School, originally founded by King Amanullah, to the Amani High School. He introduced several socio-economic changes in Afghanistan. With the help of Soviet engineers he tunnelled King Amanullah's route through the Salang Pass. Among other reforms introduced by King Amanullah, Daoud quietly abolished the custom of women using *chadri* (veil). He abrogated the Anglo-Afghan treaty of 1893, which had established the Durand Line.

King Zahir introduced several political and social reforms in his kingdom. By way of the democratization of the political system of Afghanistan, he appointed Mohammed Yousuf, a physician by profession, as Prime Minister and Minister of the Interior on 10 March 1963. Mohammed Yousuf was the first non-Pashtun Prime Minister of Afghanistan: he was a Tajik. King Zahir also gave Afghanistan a constitution on 1 October 1964. This constitution included a clause prohibiting members of the royal family from participating in state affairs, that is, from serving as Ministers, Members of Parliament, or Justices of the Supreme Court, in order to separate the Crown from the Government. Briefly, this constitution combined modern ideas with Islamic religious and political concepts.

King Zahir declared both Dari and Pashto official languages of Afghanistan. Before the constitution of 1964, Pashto, the language of the Pashtun majority, was not the official language of the country. Although King Zahir did not implement legislation concerning the establishment of political parties, he adopted several measures for developing the status of the legislature in the post-1964 period. There were, on the morrow of the constitution, a number of political parties in Afghanistan such as the Afghan Millat, Khalq-i-Afghanistan/People's Democratic Party of Afghanistan (PDPA) and Ikhwan-ul-Muslimin were formed. The PDPA's programme, published in 1966, envisaged radical socio-economic and political reforms. The party split into two factions in 1967. On 1 January 1965 Noor Muhammad Taraki (1917-79) of Ghazni, a writer by vocation, founded the Khalq (People) faction with himself as the General Secretary. Babrak Karmal of Kabul, a lawyer by profession, founded the Parcham (Flag) faction. Ikwan-ul-Muslimin also split into Hizb-i-Islami and Jamat-i-Islami.

On 17 July 1973 Daoud overthrew King Zahir Shah during his absence in Europe and seized power with the help of the Soviet-trained officers of the armed forces of Afghanistan. On 18 July he abolished the constitution of 1964 and proclaimed Afghanistan a republic with himself as President. He renounced his royal titles. He also took the offices of Prime Minister, Foreign Minister and Minister of Defence. He called his party the Milli Gurzangh, "National Revolutionary Party".

Daoud's coup was a watershed in the politics of modern Afghanistan. It overthrew the monarchical system and replaced it by the party system combining both traditional and modern elements. Unfortunately, President Daoud fell to assassins before establishing a viable order. He was a man with a vision. His tragedy was his alienation from his cousins and other able administrators of Afghanistan.

Moscow, which had gradually established its influence in Afghanistan by the early 1970s, was the first to recognize the government of Daoud. There is, however, no evidence that Moscow inspired or manipulated the coup. It wielded considerable influence in Kabul under President Daoud. It further extended the Afghan-Soviet treaty of 1931 on the occasion of the state visit of Nikolai Podgorny, President of the Presidium of the Supreme Soviet of the Soviet Union, to Afghanistan on 9-10 December 1975. In his speech on this occasion, President Daoud emphasized the importance of the treaty of 1931 as the foundation of friendship and good-neighbourliness between Afghanistan and the Soviet Union. Little did he realize then that this friendship would prove to be his own undoing and death.

The West accepted the Daoud coup as an affair that had something to do with feuds within the ruling elite of Afghanistan and Daoud's driving ambition, although several Soviet-trained officers of the armed forces of Afghanistan had been involved. However, Afghanistan's pro-Soviet tilt disturbed it greatly. But the efforts made, especially the diplomatic initiatives of Shah Mohammed Reza Pahlavi of Iran from 1974 onwards for rolling back the Soviet influence from Afghanistan, proved futile, The Shah of Iran even lent Daoud the services of experts from SAVAK, secret police of the

Shah of Iran, to streamline the security system of Afghanistan.

Daoud, who depended on the support of the local Leftists till 1976 to secure his hold over power, ultimately appeared to retrieve his position and move away from the Soviet Union. In the Loya Jirga, which he convened for the purpose of securing its approval for the draft constitution of the Republic of Afghanistan on 30 January 1977, he affirmed Afghanistan's solidatrity with the Islamic and non-aligned nations. The Loya Jirga not only approved the draft constitution providing for a presidential form of government and one party state, but also elected Daoud as president for six years. In March 1977 Daoud severed his connection with the Leftists. He replaced Soviet-trained personnel of the armed forces of Afghanistan with officers loyal to him. Thus he broke away from the Soviet-trained officers corps which had enabled him to seize power in 1973.

Apparently all this was too late, for Moscow viewed it with great concern, especially Daoud's bid to reduce Afghanistan's dependence on Soviet economic and military assistance and to diversify the sources of aid and trade. Although Moscow could not directly pressure Daoud to refrain from improving relations with the Shah of Iran, it outbid Tehran by offering further credits and committed Kabul to a long-term economic treaty on 16 April 1977.

The Soviet Government invited President Daoud along with his younger brother and adviser, Mohammed Naim, to visit the Soviet Union on 12-14 April 1977. The speech of President Nikolai Podgorny, at the banquet hold in honour of President Daoud in the Kremlin, reflected Soviet anxiety to win him. Said President Podgorny :

> You, Mr President, are well known in our country as an outstanding statesman who had made a big contribution to promoting friendship between the USSR and Afghanistan. Naturally, therefore, you are being met and received in the Soviet Union as a welcome and respected guest. Our meeting and talks in the past have invariably been marked by an atmosphere of goodwill, contributed to better mutual understanding between the parties of our two neighbouring states and stimulated further development of friendly Soviet-Afghan relations. . . . Lenin wrote that the High Afghan State was one of the first states whose representatives we gladly welcomed in Moscow and we are happy to say that the first treaty of friendship which the Afghan people concluded was with Russia. The treaty of friendship signed in 1921 as well as the treaty

on neutrality and mutual non-aggression of 1931, the protocol on whose extension we, Mr President, signed in Kabul a year and a half ago, provide a solid foundation for friendly Soviet-Afghan relations meeting the interests of the people of the two countries and the interests of peace and security.

Although Daoud had always emphasized the importance of the treaty of 1931 as the firm basis for the development of friendly and neighbourly relations between Afghanistan and the Soviet Union, he perhaps felt for the first time that this ' friendship" meant his own undoing. Unfortunately, a year later, it proved to be so.

Daoud's moves away from a pro-Soviet policy resulted in the coup of the armed forces of Afghanistan on 27 April 1978/7 Saur 1357. The radicals overthrew Daoud, who himself had overthrown the monarchy. They killed him, his brother Naim, many members of their families and close civil and and military officials. Colonel Abdul Kadir, Chairman of the *Shora-i-inqlabi*/Revolutionary Council, which assumed power, proclaimed democratic republic of Afghanistan (DRA) and abolished Daoud's constitution of 1977. The Revolutionary Council created the Khalq-Pracham coalition. It made Noor Muhammad Taraki President of the Revolutionary Council and the Prime Minister of the DRA. Except the PDPA, the Revolutionary Council allowed no other political party to function in Afghanistan. It purged all persons abolished considered undesirable in the civil and military services of the country. Above all, it reversed the efforts made by Daoud to reduce Afghanistan's dependence on the Soviet Union.

As the coup of 1973 destroyed the *ancient regime* in Afghanistan, the coup of 1978 destroyed the republican regime there.

The Soviet Union recognized the Democratic Republic of Afghanistan on 29 April 1978. It was the first to do so. There was widespread speculation concerning the Soviet role in the April/Saur revolution. Anyway the Soviet Union hailed it as a victory for Marxism-Leninism, although Karl Marx and Communism had not been mentioned in the manifesto of the PDPA.

The People's Republic of China (PRC) accepted the political change in Afghanistan and recognized the Democratic Republic of Afghanistan on 8 May 1978. But it appears to have done so with reservations for soon acute tension developed between Afghanistan and China. Beijing charged Kabul with pro-Sovietism. Kabul countered by charging Beijing with training and supplying arms to Afghan band its and allying itself with Afghanistan's enemies. Anyway Beijing did not recognize the Government of Babrak Karmal set up on 27 December 1979.

Afghanistan was among the first countries to recognize the People's Republic of China on 12 January 1950. Whenever there was a discussion of seating the PRC in the United Nations in the early 1950s, the Afghan delegation abstained. After Afghanistan and the PRC established embassy-level diplomatic relations on 19 January 1955, Afghanistan like Burma, India and the Soviet Union vigorously started advocating seating of the PRC in the UN. The Afghan delegation said in the UN General Assembly:

> We believe that any further absence of the legitimate representative of China from this Organization is not only contrary to the norms of international law, but is also not in the interest of world peace.

Zhou Enlai (1898-1976), Premier of the Council of State and Foreign Minister of the PRC, who visited Afghanistan on 19 January 1957, emphasized the contacts between China and Afghanistan from time immemorial and their common struggle for independence as the basis of mutual respect and development of relations between the two countries. He further said that the victory attained by the Afghan people in their struggle for independence inspired the Chinese people in fighting for their own independence.

Prime Minister Daoud returned the visit on 22-30 October 1957.

Afghanistan and China concluded several agreements and treaties. Notable among them was the 10-year treaty of friendship and non-aggression signed in Kabul on 25 August 1960. Simultaneously with the signing of this treaty the two countries exchanged notes terminating the treaty between Afghanistan and the Republic of China (ROC) signed in Ankara on 2 March 1944. Marshal Ch'en Yi, Vice-Premier and Foreign Minister of the PRC, who signed the treaty on behalf of the PRC, characterized it as the "crystallization of a friendship which had been tested by history and developed further on a new basis".

Afghanistan and China also signed a treaty in Beijing on 22 November 1962 to delimit their boundary. This treaty put an end to Chinese claim to northeast Afghanistan. It is interesting that China, which was inactive in the Anglo-Russian rivalry for supremacy in the Pamir region and which had not participated in the demarcation of boundaries there in the second half of the nineteenth century, has taken a special interest in the region since the early 1970s. In the 1890s, British diplomacy had sought to influence China to establish its claim to the Pamir region and assert its position there as, in the British view, delimitation of boundaries in the Pamir region without the participation of China was not of much value. The British frequently exercised their power to sustain China against Russian expansionism in Central Asia. China was never so much of a problem to the British in Central Asia as Russia was then.

China first denounced Daoud's assumption of power on 17 July 1973 as an action inspired by the Soviet Union. But after Daoud's assurances that Afghanistan would adhere to neutrality in the Chinese-Soviet dispute, it concluded several agreements with his government, including the one on economic and technical cooperation signed in Beijing on 8 December 1974.

After 27 December 1979, Beijing considered the Soviet military presence in Afghanistan a threat to its security. On 21 January 1980, Beijing put off the talks for normalization of relations with Moscow in view of the Afghan events, and it has ever since insisted on the withdrawal of Soviet troops from Afghanistan as the precondition for the solution of the Afghan problem. It has, morally and materially supported the *Mujahidin* (Doctor of Law) insurgency in Afghanistan as it has supported insurgency in other neighbouring countries like Burma and India. The Afghan insurgents, according to China, represent the people of Afghanistan and their aspirations.

Apart from the settlement of the short strip of border vide the Afghan-Chinese boundary treaty of 1962, nothing much of importance happened between the two countries. (The common border between Afghanistan and China seems to have disappeared after 1979. Perhaps, with goodwill, good neighbourliness and mutual concessions on the part of Kabul and Moscow, the principle of territorial integrity admits the legality of territorial changes.) Anyway China never had a high posture in Afghanistan: it was never in a position to extend economic aid to Afghanistan on the same scale as the Soviet Union or the United States.

With the advent of Taraki, the Soviet influence in Afghanistan developed rapidly. The Soviets looked upon this new socialist state in Asia with special favour. Moscow concluded numerous agreements with the government of Taraki, both to sustain it and to ensure the non-reversal of the revolutionary change in Afghanistan. The signing of the 20-year Treaty of Friendship, Goodneighbourliness and Cooperation by Leonid Ilyich Brezhnev and

Noor Muhammad Taraki in Moscow on 5 November 1978 brought Afghanistan closer to the Soviet Union than any of the earlier treaties concluded between them.

The treaty of 1978, which reaffirmed the aims and principles of the Afghan-Soviet treaties of 1921 and 1931, called on the two parties to "consult each other and take by agreement appropriate measures to ensure the security, independence and territorial integrity of the two countries". According to the preamble of the treaty, Kabul and Moscow concluded it for the purpose of safeguarding their security and independence. On 16 June Brezhnev declared: "We resolutely condemn the subversive activities against the Afghan revolution and shall not leave our friends, the Afghan people, who have the right to build their life the way they wish."

Taraki made Hafizullah Amin of Paghman, a teacher by profession, a Vice-President of the Revolutionary Council and a Deputy Prime Minister and Foreign Minister of the Democractic Republic of Afghanistan. In March 1979, Amin became the Minister of Defence and assumed control of the struggle against the insurgency. In July, Taraki also appointed him Prime Minister. On 14 September Amin ousted Taraki. He assumed Taraki's offices on 16 September.

Taraki, the father figure of the Marxist movement in Afghanistan, was a mere figure-head. Amin was the active head of the revolutionary regime.

Amin, an ardent Communist, seemed to emulate both Amanullah and Daoud, ardent nationalists. He had even moved his residential and operational headquarters with a small body of personal guard f.om the House of the People in central Kabul to the Tapa-i-Tajbek Palace on the south-western outskirts of the city on 20 December 1979 before his assassination on 27 December. Perhaps Amin also wanted to pursue a Yugoslavia-type foreign policy. Amin was a serious man. He faced real difficulties in the wake of attempting internal reforms particularly agrarian reforms in the country. These reforms dealt a severe blow to the feudal-patriarchal system of the country. His hard line Communism was really unpopular. He moved too fast and too soon away from the traditional socio-economic circumstances of the then Afghanistan. He seems to have been in a hurry to make revolutionary history.

When Soviet armed forces entered Afghanistan on 24 December 1979, the thrust of events Iran and in the Persian Gulf and the reversal of the Soviet position in Egypt[5] were still fresh in the minds of those who were in charge of Soviet foreign policy. Moscow also feared the collapse of the PDPA regime and the loss of revolutionary gains in Afghanistan. The Soviets perhaps believed that either Amin would be over-thrown by the anti-Marxist, anti-Soviet insurgent forces in the country or he would remain in power but pursue policies incompatible with Soviet interests there. But the real *raison d'etre* was that, like Daoud, he was becoming too independent in his way of thinking and decision, and unmanageable. He had over reached himself in his insistence on the recall of the Soviet Ambassador, A.M. Puzanov, who had apparently involved himself too directly in the internal policies of Afghanistan.

Moscow plucked Babrak Karmal of the Parcham faction of the PDPA in Czechoslowakia and sponsored him as the General Secretary of the PDPA, the President of the Revolutionary Council and the Commander of the People's Army of Afghanistan on 27 December 1979. Moscow justified its action on the plea of Kabul requesting for urgent assistance within the framework of the Afghan-Soviet treaty of 1978.

Babrak Karmal was a member of the Loya Jirga under King Zahir Shah's constitution of 1964. He first came to prominence when a small group of Leftist intellectuals demonstrated against the government of Mohammed Yousuf on 24 October 1965/3 Akrab 1342. He was a member of the Khalq-Parcham coalition, led by Taraki. Like Amin, he was a Vice-President of the Presidium of the Revolutionary Council and a Deputy Prime Minister of DRA. Taraki gave Karmal a diplomatic post in Czechoslovakia to get him out of the country. Karmal was in East Europe when Amin assumed power on 16 September 1979. He became the first non-Pashtun head of state of the Democratic Rupublic of Afghanistan.

The entry of Soviet armed forces into Afghanistan raised a vehement protest internationally. China, the United States, West Europe, Japan the Jeddah-based Islamic Conference, short for the Islamic Foreign Ministers Conference (IFMC), and the UN General Assembly (where the veto does not apply, but which lacks power to make its resolution binding) not only expressed strong dissapproval of the Soviet action but condemned it. China was the most vociferous of all nations in condemning the Soviet action. The Islamic Conference, not only condemned the Soviet action but resolved in an extraordinary session not to recognize the PDPA regime, calling on Islamic nations to break diplomatic relations with Afghanistan. It suspended the membership of Afghanistan. The United States, China and several Arab states such as Egypt and Saudi Arabia supported, and continue to support, the insurgency in Afghanistan. For Japan, which had established diplomatic relations with Afghanistan in the mid-1930s, it was more than an expression of solidarity with the United States and the West. Japan has been a leading, if not the leading, donor of financial aid for refugees from Afghanistan.

Interestingly, development in Afghanistan illustrate a shift in the US policy since the 1950s. The US policy formulations of containment of Communism now emphasize containment of Soviet expansionism and Sovietism, although the policy itself has not changed. With the emergence of the People's Republic of China as an independent actor, the policy now expresses itself in anti-Soviet Union, not anti-China terms. In the 1950s, when the United States was undertaking multilateral commitments to contain Communism, it had described the People's Republic of China as a threat to Asia.

Why did the United States involve itself in Afghanistan ? Were security and strategic interests or the honour and dignity of the United States in danger in Afghanistan? Afghanistan was not on America's doorstep. Also, the entry of Soviet armed forces into Afghanistan was not an attack on America's vital interests such as the Persian Gulf. Was it for the vindication of its fidelity to its commitments abroad. Except imposing certain measures of demonstrative disapproval, there was precious little Washington could do to oust Soviet troops from Afghanistan or counter Soviet policies there.

Afghanistan was on the very doorstep of the Soviet Union. Moscow could afford to be insensitive to international reaction, including the UN General Assembly censures, even though highly publicized debates there greatly damaged the Soviet image in the world. International reaction to the Soviet military intervention in Afghanistan no doubt surprised the Soviet leaders. They perhaps had expected little or no opposition from outside. The determination as well as ramification of Afghan resistance went beyond the calculations of Soviet strategists. Soviet experience of the *Bashmachi* resistance in Central Asia in the 1920s was really not applicable to the *Mujahidin* resistance in Afghanistan. The two situations were quite different. For instance, the British government could not help the Basmachis as the American government has helped the Mujahidins. Diplomatically the Soviet action caused them great embarrassment It gave a considerable setback to Soviet relations with its allies. It alienated the Soviet Union from the non-aligned and Afro-Asian countries. Moscow has not yet been able to bolster its shattered prestige especially in parts of the Muslim world.

On 14 May 1980 Karmal made proposals for political talks with Afghanistan's neighbours Iran and Pakistan to settle mutual differences. The proposals included a US guarantee not to conduct subversive activity inside Afghanistan. Karmal said that acceptance of his proposals would lead to the withdrawal of Soviet troops from his country and an unravelling of the tangle in Afghanistan.

During his visit to Moscow from 8 to 11 December 1980 Karmal underlined the basic objective of the foreign policy of Afghanistan as the consolidation of friendship and cooperation with the Soviet Union and other Socialist states. The joint statement, signed by Leonid Brezhnev and Babrak Karmal in Moscow on 15 October 1980 and issued on 19 October, said:

> The Afghan side expressed profound gratitude for the all-round assistance and support rendered by the Soviet people to the Democratic Republic of Afghanistan in the latter's struggle against the counter-revolutionary intervention from outside, against imperialist interference in Afghanistan's internal affairs, for the implementation of the objectives and aims of the April revolution, for building in Afghanistan a new society based on equality and social justice.
>
> The Soviet side declared that in this struggle the people of the Democratic Republic of Afghanistan and its Government can continue to count on the Soviet people....

The joint statement described the Afghan-Soviet treaty of 1978 as the basic of Afghan-Soviet relations.

On 23 February 1981, in his report to the opening session of the Twenty-sixth Congress of the CPSU in Mocow, Brezhnev declared that the Soviet Union would withdraw its troops from Afghanistan following complete cessation of outside interference in the country and receipt of dependable, international guarantees that there would be no interference in Afghanistan. He wanted the guarantees included in the agreements between Afghanistan and Iran and Pakistan. "Such is the fundamental position of the Soviet Union and we keep to it firmly", he said.

Yuri Andropov not only reiterated this Soviet stand but also thought of ensuring the Soviet security along the Soviet-Afghan border. Konstantin Chernenko had in his address in Frunze, Kirghiz SSR, in August 1979 (he was then Secretary of the Central Committee of the CPSU) predicted the doom of the forces of reaction and imperialism in the event of their interfering in the internal affairs of Afghanistan.

Mikhail Sergei Gorbachev has maintained the position of the Soviet Union on Afghanistan first stated by Brenzhnev. Again, like Brenzhnev, he has said that the people of Afghanistan have embarked on a road to build their own society and that it is their right to do so.

On 12 December 1986, in his speech at the dinner held in the Kremlin in honour of Najibullah, General Secretary of the People's Democratic Party of Afghanistan, Gorbachev said :

…We will not abandon our southern neighbour to a difficult situation. This is a position of principle. We have no intention to leave for long our troops in Afghanistan which were sent there on the request of its government. And we have already confirmed this by the withdrawal of six regiments. I want to repeat once again : the withdrawal of troops can be expedited as soon as a just settlement around Afghanistan is achieved.

On 27 February 1981 Brezhnev and Karmal again emphasized the need for a political settlement of the issue of Afghanistan on the basis of the proposals of 14 May 1980, the Afghan-Soviet statement of 16 October 1980 and the Soviet proposal of 23 Febrnary 1981. On 20 December 1982 Karmal offered direct talks with Iran and Pakistan.

However, despite the quite helpful United Nations' indirect "proximity" talks on the issue with Afghanistan and its neighbours since 1982, there is yet no solution of the Afghan problem. Even the great expectations aroused by the Super Power summits between General Secretary Mikhail Gorbachov and President Ronald Reagan in Geneva and Reykjavik on 19-20 November 1985 and on 10-11 October 1986 respectively have come to naught.

The crucial point underscoring the issue is the question of the withdrawal of Soviet troops from Afghanistan. Interestingly, the Soviet stand in the matter reveals a definite, historical pattern. Moscow insists on the acceptance of the Afghan and Soviet proposals before the withdrawal of its troops from Afghanistan. That is, Soviet troops would be withdrawn from Afghanistan as soon as Afghanistan is able to defend its frontiers and safeguard its security. In Moscow's view, the question is not one of Soviet troops in Afghanistan, their number or their withdrawal, but one of statecraft. According to Moscow, Soviet troops are there under the Afghan-Soviet treaty of 1978 and the

USSR may either bring its troops to Afghanistan or recall them according to the contingency of its treaty commitments. Washington insists on the withdrawal of Soviet troops from Afghanistan before any agreement concerning the form of government in Afghanistan may be initiated. That is, any agreement on the settlement of the problem of Afghanistan must first provide for the withdrawal of Soviet troops from there.

A change in the attitudes of the Soviet Union and the United States is necessary for creating effective negotiating positions. The US offer to the United Nations to act as a guarantor to a settlement of the issue, including an end to aid to the Afghan inpurgants and the Soviet willingness to withdraw its troops from Afghanistan marks a significant change in the American and Soviet attitudes.

The replacement of Babrak Karmal as the General Secretary of the PDPA by Najibullah of Pakhtiya, a physician by profession and chief of the secret police up to December 1985, on 4 May 1986 ostensibly on his own request, marked very significant developments in the DRA. On 23 November, Haji Muhammad Samkanai of Pakhtiya, a civil servant by profession, became the Acting President of the DRA. Until then he was a Vice-President of the Revolutionary Council. All this reflects the new mood, the new thinking of the Soviet leadership on the question of Afganistan since the Twenty-seventh Congress of the CPSU in March 1985.

Najibullah is a Parchami, but he is also a Pashtun. He may be able to secure the cooperation of both the Pashtun Khalqis as well as the Pashtun rebels. Since assuming leadership of the Party, he has been endeavouring for national reconciliation in the country. He is now broadening the structure of his regime in order to enlist non-party cooperation. If necesarry, he may even join the Khalqi faction, the major element of the PDPA. Among the Pashtuns tribalism itself is ideology.

The Soviet Union has been developing Afghanistan on the Mongolian model. The Soviet bloc's economic oganization, CMEA (Council for Mutual Economic Assistance), admitted Afghanistan as an observer on 19 June 1980 even as it had admitted Mongolia, the first Marxist state in Asia. Since then, Afghanistan has undergone the process of economic integration into the CMEA. By drawing Afghanistan into the CMEA, the Soviet Union seeks to shape its economic relations. Direct contacts between Afghanistan and the Central Asian Tajik, Uzbek and Turkmen republics has already acquired much momentum.

Afghnistan has traditionally been an area where Russia exerted influence. The history of Afghan-Russian relations reveals that the Soviet Government may not tolerate the transformation of Afghanistan into a base of aggression against the Soviet Union. It will not withdraw from Afghanistan, it has said so time and again, unless all external interference in that country's internal affairs or support extended to the rebels ends. It will spare no effort—military, economic and political—to maintain its position there. It is so because of geo-politics, not ideology. Of course, Moscow will need international diplomacy to recognize the legitimacy of the regime in Kabul as well as its own position of predominance in Afghanistan.

Soviet control of Afghanistan, however, has fundamentally changed the situation east of the Khaibar Pass. It has changed the strategic map of South Asia. Even though the aim of the Soviet military move in Afghanistan might have been to secure its southern flank against a perceived threat, it certainly has lengthened the shadow of Soviet military power over South Asia. Now the question is : Will the Soviets remain on the Khaibar with the Indus River in front or organize insurrection east of it ? Even if Soviet troops do not advance east of the Khaibar, their very presence in Afghanistan can lead to constant upheaval and ruinous expense. The Soviet presence in Afghanistan has brought the Soviet Union to India's doorstep. Have the leaders of India reflected on this in the context of India's own security ? If not, they ought to do so. For apart from the long common history and cultural and ethnical affinities between Afghanistan and India, the geographical location of Afghanistan is of special importance from the point of India's security environment. It was always the ambition of Russia to extend its influence southwards and have a a common frontier with India, as with China and Iran. The Soviet ambition seems to be the same. Or is it not ?

Both India and Pakistan find the Soviet presence in Afghanistan in their national interests—India in the context of its problem with Pakistan and Pakistan in the context of its problem with Afghanistan and India. Anything can happen any time in the scenario of Pakistan's relations with its neighbours. Pakistan can play a Soviet card and resile from its position as a frontline state in respect of Afghanistan. Also, Pakistan, in its national interest, may not consider it prepostrous to involve the United States even in a war and so on. If the preservation and strengthening of a peaceable and stable South Asia are Soviet and US goals, then, before or simutaneously attempting a solution of the Afghan question, the United States not only as great powers but also as superpower, must first seek rapprochement between India and Pakistan. Normal relations between India and Pakistan are imperative for peace and stability in the region.

The Soviet presence in Afghanistan may also enable the Soviet Union to become the mistress of West Asia. Of course, Iran is not yet at its disposal. The British control of Afghanistan had forced Persia to maintain a balance between Britain and Russia. Will not the Soviet control of Afghanistan force Iran to balance itself between the Soviet Union and the West? The Soviets have a military footing in Afghanistan, which the British never had. Russia was always aware that the paramount power in Persia depended on command of the Persian Gulf. The Soviet Union now has commanding position not only in the Persian Gulf but also the Indian Ocean, which Russia never did. However, even as the unwillingness of the West to help Afghanistan in the 1950s was the main factor in compelling it to look to the Soviet Union for help, the attitude of the West not to recognize the present regime in Kabul may result in a development which did not come about even with the emergence of the USSR as the dominant influence in Afghanistan during the 1960s-1970s.

At this point the question may be asked : Will history repeat itself, and will Afghanistan again be a truly independent nation ? Or will jet fighters and helicopter gunships accomplish what artillery and machine guns did not ? The Afghans once regarded their country as the "fortress of Asia" and the "axis in the balance of peace", despite limits to its sovereignty. Now they do not seem to be the masters even of their destiny. No foreign power had ever succeeded in subjugating Afghanistan. Will it now find subjugation inescapable ? As in 1839-43 and 1878-79, a section of the Afghans are now resisting foreign intervention. Will they succeed this time too ? Of course, the question is : Are the Mujahidin the same or are they different from the followers of Dost Muhammad and Abdur Rahman ? However, even if they do succeed, they may find it to be a precarious independence.

Afghanistan and the Soviet Union have maintained the closest connection since 1979. The Soviets have taken long term measures to consolidate their position in Afghanistan. They have built a bridge, officially opened on 12 May 1982, across the frontier river Amu Darya at Termez to link Afghanistan with Soviet Central Asia and strengthen economic ties between the two countries. They have established a basic civil and military infra- structure in Afghanistan. Above all, they have trained Afghan forces to defend the country in the event of the withdrawal of Soviet troops from there.

The Afghan Revolution was not a revolution like the American (1974), the French (1792), the Russian (1917) and the Chinese (1949) revolutions. Anyway it marked a movement away from feudalism in Afghanistan. And whatever may happen in Afghanistan politically, it will never remain the same economically and socially.

4

MONGOLIA 1921—1945

The Mongolian revolutionaries, who, on the eve of their revolution cast their lot with Soviet Russia, pledged their alliance by concluding a treaty in Moscow on 5 November 1921. Sukhe Bator was one of the two Khalkhas who established the first "revolutionary circles" in Mongolia ; Khorloogiin Choibalsan was the other. He had also been one of the "Khalkha Seven" to enter Soviet Russia and request Soviet help in July-August 1920 ; Bodo, D. Chakdorzhav, Kho. Choibalsan, Donzan, D. Doksom and Lama D. Losol were the other six,

According to the preamble to the Mongolian-Soviet, treaty "a sincere desire to promote free concord and cooperation between their two peoples" guided the Mongolian and Soviet sides in their relations with each other. The treaty provided for mutual recognition of the two governments of Mongolia and Soviet Russia. The Soviet Government recognized the Mongolian Government as the only legal authority of Mongolia, and the Mongolian Government recognized the Soviet Government as the only legal authority of Russia. For Mongolia it was the first treaty, the first political convenant, concluded on an equal basis. The two governments established diplomatic missions in each other's country.

Each side undertook to prevent formation of organizations and groups hostile to the other side from carrying on any kind of activity on its territory. After the signing of the treaty the Soviets organized the armed forces of Mongolia and trained its troops. The first group of Soviet military instructors included D.I. Kosich (leader), A.O. Petrov and N.S. Sorkin. Actually Kosich, a member of the Revolutionary Military Council of the Fifth Red Army, served as the chief of staff of the Mongolian army. Soviet military instructors remained in Mongolia even after the departure of Soviet troops from there in early 1925.

The Mongolian-Soviet treaty of 1921 laid the foundation of close cooperation between the two countries. The two sides accorded each other the most favoured-nation treatment in their mutual relations. The Mongolian-Soviet trade agreement concuded in 1923 established economic relations on equal basis between the two countries.

When the Chinese came to know of the Soviet-Mongolian treaty of 1921, they raised the question of its existence with A.K. Paikes, Soviet envoy in Peking. Paikes first denied its existence. When he ultimately confirmed it, he said that it was perfectly legitimate for Moscow and Urga to conclude it. He also said that the Soviet-Mongolian treaty did not violate the principle of Chinese sovereignty over Mongolia. The Chinese felt this ploy of Soviet diplomacy to be similar to the ploy of Tsarist diplomacy after the conclusion of the Russian-Monogolian agreement of 1912 whose result was to the disadvantage of China. The Chinese were not for another outcome of that sort concerning Mongolia.

Nevertheless Yen Hui-ch'ing, foreign minister of China, sent the following protest note to Paikes on 1 May 1992 :

According to the recent report of General Li Yuan on the subject of the Russo-Mongolian treaty, we asked you about this matter when you first arrived in Peking and you replied that it was entirely untrue. However, during a recent conversation with you, I again put the question to you, owing to the recent publication by the papers of the text of the treaty, and you admitted the truth of this report.

The Soviet Government has repeatedly declared to the Chinese Government that all previous treaties made between the Russian Government and China shall be null and void, that the Soviet Government renounces all encroachments of Chinese territory and all concessions within China and that the Soviet Government will unconditionally and for ever return what has been forcibly seized from China by the former Imperial Russian Government and the bourgeoise. Now the Soviet Government has suddenly gone back on its own word and, secretly and without any right, concluded a treaty with Outer Mongolia. Such action on the part of the Soviet Government is similar to the policy the former Imperial Russian Government assumed towards China.

It must be observed that Outer Mongolia is a part of Chinese territory and as such has long been recognized by all countries. In secretly concluding a treaty with Outer Mongolia, the Soviet

Government has not only broken faith with its previous declaration, but also violates all principles of Justice.

The Chinese Government finds it difficult to tolerate such an action, and therefore we solemnly lodge a protest with you to the effect that any treaty secretly concluded between the Soviet Government and Outer Mongolia will not be recognized by the Chinese Government.

Expcept protesting, there was nothing else that China could do in the matter that.

Thus in 1921, as in 1689, 1727 and 1915, Mongolia continued to remain an important factor in Sino-Soviet relations. Indeed, the question of Mongolia's political status constituted one of the obstacles in the conclusion of the Sino-Soviet treaty signed in Peking on 31 May 1924. Although Chinese authority had disappeared from Mongolia after the summer of 1921, the Sino-Soviet treaty, which declared null and void all previous Chinese-Russian treaties and pledged to replace them by new treaties on the basis of justice, equality and reciprocity accepted the facade of Chinese sovereignty over Mongolia and recognized it as part of China :

The Government of the Union of Soviet Socialist Republics recognizes that Outer Mongolia is an integral part of the Republic of China and respects China's sovereignty therein.

The Sino-Soviet treaty stated the recognition of Chinese sovereignty over Mongolia only as a principle, which might not be honoured. Perhaps the Soviet Union agreed to Chineses sovereignty over Mongolia because it was then in the Soviet interest to do so, especially in the context of the establishment of diplomatic relations with China. It was, therefore, necessary for the Soviet Government to pursue such a policy. Elimination of any impression of imperialism or suspicion of great power intentions towards China was more important for Soviet diplomacy than ever before.[1] However, Soviet attitude towards Mongolia remained ambiguous. The statement of Georgi Vasilyevich Chicherin, People's Commissar for Foreign Affairs of the USSR, on the occasion is interesting :

We recognize Mongolia as part of the Republic of China, but we also recognize its autonomy in so far-reaching a sense that we regard it not only as independent of China in its internal affairs but also as capable of running its foreign policy independently.

The Chinese will never forgive the Soviets for detaching Mongolia from China and eventually converting it into a Moscow-oriented people's republic.

The first session of the Great People's Khural[2] on 26 November 1924 proclaimed Mongolia the Mongolian People's Republic (MPR). The Mongolian Government renamed Urga and called it Ulan Bator meaning "Red Hero". Later, the Mongols drafted a constitution for themselves on the pattern of the Soviet constitution. Article 1 of the Constitution stated :

> All Mongolia is henceforth proclaimed to be a sovereign people's republic of which all the high organs of state of power belonged to the working people, and all affairs of state are decided by the Great People's Khural and its elected government.[3]

The historical significance of the first Mongolian constitution was that it set the stage for the adoption of the path of non-capitalist development by Mongolia.

In the early 1930s Japan began to advance towards Mongolia and Siberia. The Kwantung Army of Japan invanded Manchuria on 18 September 1931, and the Chahar region of Inner Mongolia in 1934. It established the state of "Manchu Kuo" in the occupied territory in February 1932. The state of Manchukuo comprised Manchuria plus parts of Inner Mongolia. Both the Mongolian People's Republic (MPR) and the Union of Soviet Socialist Republics (USSR) saw in this development a threat to Mongolia and Siberia. The USSR, however, tried to maintain friendly relations with Japan. The Soviet Government even turned the Chinese Eastern Railway (CER) to the government of Manchukuo in 1935. But the Japanese threat to the Mongolian borders went on increasing instead of decreasing. On 1 March 1936 Josef Visarionovich Stalin stated to Roy Howard of the Associated Press of America that the USSR would help the MPM in the event of a Japanese invasion. He said :

> Should Japan venture to attack the Mongolian People's Republic and encroach upon its independence, we will help (it)...We will help the MPM just as we helped it in 1921."

On 12 March, despite the Soviet desire to maintain good

relations with Japan, the MPM and the USSR signed in Ulan Bator a 10-year pact of mutual assistance which provided for military aid in the event of an attack on the MPR or the the USSR by a third country. Article 3 of the treaty provided for the stationing of troops of one party on the territory of the other.

Peking lodged a protest with Moscow that the Soviet action in concluding the treaty with Outer Mongolia was a breach of its pledge to recognize it as part of China and constituted not merely a violation of the stipulations of the Chinese-Soviet treaty of 1924 but also an infringement of the sovereignty of China. It said that the whole of Outer Mongolia, including Uryanghai, formed part of its territory.

Uryanghai was part of the Mongol land up to 1911. The Russian government made it a protectorate on 11 April 1914. The Soviet Government abolished the protectorate over it. It changed its name to Tuva and proclaimed its independence as a "people's republic" on 23 September 1921. The town Uryanghai became Kyzyl. The Tuvan People's Republic (TPR) entered into mutual recognition of independence with the Mongolian People's Republic (MPR) in 1926. When the Soviet Union went to war with Germany on 22 June 1941, it immediately declared war against Germany. On 11 October 1944 the Soviet Union annexed the Tuvan People's Republic and incorporated it into the RSFSR as an autonomuos region. Owing to its geographical location, it is of considerable strategic importance to the Soviet Union. China still claims it as Chinese territory.

Mao Tse-tung (1893-1976) of the Communist Party of China (CPC) also considered Mongolia part of China. In an interview with Edgar Snow of the United States of America on 16 July 1936, he said that when the people's revolution had been victorious in China, the Outer Mongolian Republic would return to the fold of the Chinese federation at its own will.[4]

Legally, the Soviet Union's alliance with Mongolia over the head of China was in violation of the stipulations of the Chinese-Soviet treaty of 1924. However, Mongolia was too important for the Soviet Union to give up connection with it for mere theoretical considerations. Its geographical position as a buffer, and as a military deployment area, against Japan was of supreme importance.

Although Japan had full knowledge of the treaty between Moscow and Ulan Bator, the Japanese military forces attacked the Mongolian border guards in the area of Lake Khasan in 1938 and at Nomonhan on the Khalkin Gol River, near the trijunction of Inner Mongolia, militarists thought that the Soviet Union would not be able to provide necessary assistance to Mongolia. Perhaps they meant the invasion of Mongolia to test the Soviet military strength. Anyway, on 31 May 1939, Moscow warned Tokyo that, in accordance with the Soviet-Mongolian pact of 1936, it regarded the Mongolian borders as its own. On the initiative of the Mongolian Government, Soviet military forces entered Mongolia to fight the Japanese forces. By 30 August 1939 Soviet-Mongolian forces under the command of Lieutenant-General (later Field Marshal) Georgi Konstantinovich Zukhov (1896-1974) had achieved a decisive victory over the Japanese forces.

Mongolia was not a member of the League of Nations. It remained neutral during the European war of 1939-45. It entered the eastern war at the very end. On 11 August 1945, two days after the Soviet Union's declaration of war against Japan, it followed suit and, together with the Soviet Union, it fought against Japan a week before the Japanese surrender on 2 September 1945. Soviet troops remained in Mongolia until 1956.

On 8 February 1945 Prime Minister Winston S. Churchill (1874-1965) and President Franklin D. Roosevelt (1882-1945) made a deal with Marshal J.V. Stalin (1879-1953) at Yalta in the Crimea. In return for Soviet participation in the war against Japan, they agreed to preserve the *status quo* in Outer Mongolia and interpret it to mean its independence.[5] A clause of the agreement required the concurrence of Generalissimo Chiang Kai-shek (1886-1975) of China with the fulfilment of the conditions relating to Outer Mongolia. President Roosevelt was "to take measures to obtain this concurrence on advice from Marshal Stalin". He undertook to assume the responsibility of persuading Chiang Kai-shek to accept this position. He also persuaded Stalin to conclude a treaty of friendship with China.

China had no representative at Yalta. Of course, at a dinner meeting with Roosevelt in Cairo on 23 November 1943, Chiang Kai-shek had raised the question of the return of Outer Mongolia to China. He also wrote that China should win back Outer Mongolia. There is also the interesting, although intriguing hypothesis: What would have been Mongolia's position at Yalta if the Japanese had taken it, or disaffected its inhabitants, as a part of their programme of pau-Mongolain unity ? Would not it have come out as part of China ? Of course, the Japanese conception of pan-Manchukuo and Mongolia, on 11 May 1939. Perhaps the Japanese Mongolian unity was so vague.

China was not in position to reject and/or ignore the American advice. China and the Soviet Union concluded a treaty of friendship and alliance in Moscow on 14 August 1945.[6] The agreement, designed to implement the Sino-Soviet treaty of 1945, provided for the independence of Mongolia from China to be determined by plebiscite. The plebiscite held on 20 October 1945 resulted in a vote for the independence of Mongolia outside the political framework of China, China accepted, even though grudgingly, the Mongolian people's vote for independence. It formally recognized the Mongolian People's Republic on 5 January 1945 and agreed to establish diplomatic relations with it on 13 February 1946.

At that time conditions in Chungking were not conducive for China and Mongolia to exchange diplomatic missions. Later, China used the border incident on the MPR-Sinkiang border near the town of Peitashan northeast of Urumchi in June 1947 as pretext for delay. Had the exchange of diplomatic missions between the Republic of China and (ROC)the Mongolian People's (MPR) made any difference in the situation ? The rulers of China did not seem to abandon their policy of annexing Mongolia. According to the Mongols, they continually provoked incidents on the MPR-Sinkiang border in order to slander the MPR in the eyes of the United Nations and thereby to prevent it from being accepted into the family of nations. Mongolia had the right to become a founding member of the United Nations by virtue of its direct participation in World War II.

Moscow changed the designation of its diplomatic representative at Ulan Bator to minister. This designation changed to that of ambassador after the conclusion of the Treaty of Friendship, Alliance and Mutual Assistance by the People's Republic of China (PRC) and the Union of Soviet Socialist Republics (USSR) in Moscow on 14 February 1950.

The circumstances of World War II not only removed Mongolia from the Chinese sphere of influence but also brought it within the Soviet sphere of influence. The Mongolian and Soviet Governments concluded a 20-year treaty of friendship and mutual assistance and an agreement on econcmic and cultural cooperation in Moscow on 27 February 1946. The Soviet-Mongolian treaty of 1946 reproduced verbatim the text of the Soviet-Mongolian pact of 1936.

Thus China and the Soviet Union were then the only countries to recognize Mongolia as a sovereign state although the Roosevelt-Stalin deal had implied Allied recognition of Mongolian independence from China. India established diplomatic relations with Mongolia after its own independence on 15 August 1947. After the confirmation of Mongolian independence in the treaty of friendship, alliance and mutual assistance signed by the PRC and the USSR in Moscow on 14 February 1950, important changes took place in the position of Mongolia. Its international position consolidated greatly. Of course, it received widespread recognition and its international relations expanded mainly after its entry into the United Nations on 27 October 1961, which marked the definite confirmation of its independent statehood. This ended the isolation of Mongolia. Ever since the seventeenth century Mongolia had been limited in its freedom of action by the necessity of taking one or other of its immediate neighbours—China or Russia—as a protector.

For gaining entry into the United Nations the MPR certainly owed a lot to the strategy of keeping the People's Republic of China (PRC) out of it. The Republic of China (based on Taiwan) as a permanent member of the UN Security Council had refrained from exercising its veto, as *quid pro quo*, on 27 October 1961. Today Mongolia's participation in international relations is very ful.

NOTES AND REFERENCES

1. The Sino-Soviet treaty also pledged to return to China the Chinese Eastern Railway (CER), the section of the Trans-Siberian Railway that went through Manchuria to the Pacific coast, immediately after the organization of a unified Chinese government that could guarantee from its falling into the hands of imperialists particularly Japan.

2. The great People's Khural is the supreme legislative body (parliament) of the MPR and, therefore, the highest organ of state power in Mongolia.

The *Khural* is the traditional assembly of Mongol clan leaders for consultation and discussion of important matters. Chinggis Khan used it for unifying the Mongols.

3. *Red Star Over China*. New York, 1937, p. 96 ; rev. ed., 1968, p. 110. This implied the self-determination of the Mongols, Tibetans and Turks of Mongolia, Tibet and Xinjiang in accordance with the objectives of the Communist Party of China.

4. The Yalta agreements also pledged to the Soviet Union the return of the Chinese Eastern Railway (CER), which Stalin had relinquished to Japan, instead of China, in 1935. In 1952, Stalin returned the CER to the People's Republic of China after rather extensive negotiations.

5. The Sino-Soviet treaty of 1945 was to remain in force for thirty years, after which it would automatically be renewed every five years unless one of the parties cancelled it.

6. The treaty was seen as a victory for Chiang Kai-shek. Mao Tse-tung found it shocking. It committed Soviet moral support and aid in military supplies and other material resources to be "entirely given to the the Nationalist Government as the centeral government of China".

5

MONGOLIA, 1945-

The Mongolian People's Republic (MPR) hailed the revolution in China as a true revolution and the proclamation and the establishment of the People's Republic of China (PRC) on 1 October 1949 as a true democracy. The Mongolian Peoples Revolutionary Party (MPRP)[1] and the Mongolian intellectuals expressed great admiration for revolutionary China. Not a few sincerely believed, it seems, that given the choice, the MPR would befriend the PRC rather than the USSR.

The MPR sought to establish close ties with the PRC despite its sympathetic attitude, as in 1911-13, to the movement for Inner Mongolian autonomy in 1945-48. It recognized the PRC on 5 October 1949. When it did so, the Republic of China (ROC), then in Guangzhou, cancelled its recognition of the independence of the MPR. Mongolia was the ninth nation after the Soviet Union, and the second Asian nation after North Korea, to recognize the PRC. The PRC, together with the USSR, confirmed Mongolian independence in the Treaty of Friendship, Alliance and Mutual Assistance signed by them in Moscow on 14 February 1950. Beijing and Ulan Bator established diplomatic relations in July 1950.

Although before the triumph of the revolution in China, Mao had always thought of securing the restoration of Outer Mongolia (i.e., MPR) to China, he agreed to Mongolian independence with Stalin in the hope that the People's Republic of China would be able to benefit from the changed situation in Siberia and East Asia. The relative status of China and Mongolia had perhaps changed more than that of any other two nations since the Hans and Mongols shook off Manchu authority in 1911. China, legally the suzerain of Mongolia up to 1945, had not even had a representative in Mongolia after 1921.

During the presence of a delegation from Beijing headed by Zhou Enlai, Prime Minister and Foreign Minister of the State Council of the PRC in Moscow from 17 August to 22 September 1952, Yumzhagiin Tsedenbal, First Secretary of the MPRP and Chairman of the Presidium of the Great People's Khural since the passing away of Kho. Choibalsan on 26 January 1952, had talks with the leaders of the PRC and the USSR. He met Mao on 29 September 1952. He had met Stalin on 5 September 1952. To impress the Mongols, the People's Republic of China also decided to lend support to Mongolia as to other neighbouring countries like North Korea and North Vietnam The Chinese and the Mongols also extended the broad gauge trans-Mongolian railway line southward from Ulan Bator to Zamyn Ude on the Mongolian[2] Chinese' frontier and to Chining, a junction point sixty miles inside China. Completed in 1956, it is connected with Beijing. During the Cultural Revolution (1966-76), the Chinese tore up the broad gauge and laid their own narrow gauge tracks to Zamyn Ude.

On 4 October 1952, the PRC and MPR signed in Beijing a 10-year agreement to establish trade and cultural relations between the two countries. The agreement was renewable for a further 10-year period unless either party gave a year's notice of termination. Article 2 of the agreement stated:

> On the basis of the present Agreement and with the aim of implementing it, concrete agreements will be signed separately between agencies of the People's Republic of China and the Mongolian People's Republic concerned with questions of economics, trade, culture and education.

Under the agreement China supplied labour to Mongolia free of allcost as evidence of its friendship. The first group of Chinese labourers, construction workers and farmers arrived in Mongolia in May 1955 and the last group on May 1961, the total reaching 20,000 or more.

One of the first projects that China helped execute in Mongolia under the agreement was the construction of a dam on the Tarani River to supply electric power and to divert water for irrigation purposes and thus lay the basis for cultivation in the area surrounding the historic city of Karakoram. The Chinese labourers built irrigation channels across the traces in the ground of the medieval fields in Karakoram.

The Sino-Mongolia agreement of 1952 fulfilled, in a way, Mao's hope of China's return to Mongolia.

The MPR and PRC signed a treaty of friendship and mutual assistance in Ulan Bator on 31 May 1960. Zhou Enlai offered the MPR a steel plant at Darkhan and a three-hundred-thousand man labour force. Ulan Bator did not take Zhou's offer. And no Chinese ever worked on the Darkhan project. However, the proposal represented the PRC's most important attempt to move Mongolia away from the USSR and orient it towards China.

The joint communique signed by Yumzhagiin Tsedenbal and Zhou Enlai expressed, among other things, support for Soviet efforts to ease international tension This had a special significance in view of the growing differences between the PRC and the USSR over such international issues as the border clashes between China and India, etc. The MPR supported the Soviet policy on the question of representation of the PRC at the United Nations on 25 October 1971.

The PRC celebrated the 800th birth anniversary of Chinggis Khan, the great ancestor of the Mongols, in May 1962. Historians of the People's Republic of China extolled his work and ascribed to him a progressive role in the history of China and other countries. According to the *Renmin Ribao*, Chinggis Khan erased the borders between nationalities and re-established the multinational state of China for the first time since the time of the Han and Tang dynasties. The PRC historians do not consider Mongol rule in China as the rule of aliens who invaded China.

The PRC had built an impressive blue and yellow mausoleum, a magnificent tomb, on a hillside in Ezen Khoro, northeast of Ulanhot City in the Ordos region of Inner Mongolia in the 1950s and placed Chinggis Khan's relics in it. The Red Guards destroyed this mausoleum during the Cultural Revolution. China later rebuilt the Chinggis Khan Temple. According to the Chinese, Chinggis Khan lies buried there. This, however, is an error. Mongol tradition does not permit worship of deceased persons at the actual place of burial. There is the location of only the cult of Chinggis Khan as a god, not his tomb, in the Ordos region. The Mongols took the body of Chinggis Khan to the holy Mount Bur Khan Khaldun at the sources of the Kerulan and Onon rivers, near his birth place Dulun Boldog, and buried it there. The exact location of the place of burial is unknown. It was a Mongol custom to hide the burial place of their rulers. Trees were planted on it to make the place indistinguishable from the surrounding country. Those actually involved in the burial were killed, so that within a relatively short time, the precise location of the burial place was forgotten.

Anyway the celebration of the anniversary of Chinggis Khan enabled the Chinese to declare themselves heirs of Chinggis Khan. It also provided impetus to Mongolian nationalist sentiment. The MPR celebrated the 800th anniversary of Chinggis Khan on 31 May 1962.

Moscow felt that Beijing was playing up the role of Chinggis Khan with a view to strengthening its own influence in Mongolia. Soviet scholars vehemently attacked Chinggis Khan during the same month in which Ulan Bator celebrated the anniversary of Chinggis Khan. As a result, Mongolia withdrew official approval of the celebration of the anniversary of the great national hero of the Mongols. On 10 September 1962 Ulan Bator denounced D. Tomor Ochir, secretary of the Central Committee of the Mongolian People's Revolutionary Party (CCMPRP) and organizer of the celebrations of the anniversary of Chinggis Khan.

On 8 January 1963 a Soviet delegation headed by L.P. Ilyichev, secretary of the Central Committee of the Communist Party of Soviet Union (CCCPSU), visited Ulan Bator to attend a meeting of the CCMPRP. At an extraordinary session of the MPRP, Yumzhagiin Tsedenbal condemned the leaders of the PRC as dogmatists and adventurists while Ilyichev condemned the misinterpretation of the role of Chinggis Khan in history. Ilyichev asked: "Why are the bloody and devastating expeditions of Chinggis Khan being exalted?" The reason, he said, lay in the fact that the PRC sought, in a camouflaged but subtle manner, to further its long term territorial aims with an eye to Mongolia and the Soviet Union.

The Chinese responded to the charges, saying that the Golden Horde of Chinggis Khan had given the Russians an opportunity to become acquainted with a superior culture (that is, Chinese culture) and lift their level of social development.

After long negotiations, the PRC and the MPR concluded in Beijing on 16 December 1962 a treaty to delimit their 2,000 kilometre long common boundary. The leaders of the PRC described the conclusion of the treaty as "a major task of historic significance". This treaty was perhaps Beijing's last attempt to regain influence in the MPR though the MPR's close alliance with the USSR had been so evident from its joining CMEA on 7 June 1962. Anyway the treaty did seen to relieve the tension then developing between the two countries.

As in the case of the boundary treaty between China and Afghanistan, China concluded this treaty with Mongolia in the context of its boundary dispute with the USSR. Like China's boundary treaties with Burma and Nepal signed in Beijing on 1 October 1960 and 5 October 1961 respectively, the boundary treaty between Beijing and Ulan Bator was advantageous to Mongolia, inasmuch as it restored to it territory it had claimed in the Altai region in the western sector, where the two countries had clashed in the summer of 1947. Before the conclusion of the treaty of 1962, the Mongolian-Chinese borders had been arbitrary. Chinese maps had consistently shown the Chinese-Mongolian boundary as undemarcated.

Yumzhagiin Tsedenbal, who (accompanied by Sanjiin Bata, D. Chimiddorj, Nyamyn Jagvaral, Puntsagiin Shagdarsuren and Sandagiin Sosorbaram) visited Beijing to sign the treaty on 25-27 December 1962, defended Nikita Khrushchev in his speech at a mass rally held in his honour against the Chinese criticism of Khrushchev's handling of the Cuban missile crisis of 16 October 1962. He said:

> When frantic US imperialists, attempting to strangle the Cuban revolution by force, decided with swords in hand to attack free socialist Cuba, thus posing a direct threat of world thermonuclear war, the leader of the Soviet Union, in co-operation with the leaders of the Republic of Cuba, took resolute, flexible action and removed the catastrophic danger over all mankind. This outcome ...is great victory for the policy of peace of the whole Socialist camp. The Cuban events show that it is possible and necessary to make wise compromises in our policies after objectively considering the whole situation and specific conditions in international life.

Zhou Enlai and other Chinese leaders present on the occasion heard without comment this speech by Yumzhagiin Tsedenbal supporting Soviet policy towards Cuba. While Yumzhagiin Tsedenbal considered Khrushchev's decision to take the nuclear missiles back to the Soviet Union from Cuba as an act of statesmanship and high responsibility, the Chinese leaders did everything to make it appear as amounting to a repudiation of the Marxist-Leninist ideology. Allegedly, among other matters such as the U-2 incident, Khrushchev lost his position over the issue of his taking back the nuclear missiles from Cuba.

The MPR could have benefited from its close connection with both the PRC and the USSR, but in the differences that existed between them in the 1960s, it sided with the USSR. During the period of Chinese Soviet friendship and cooperation from 1952 to 1957, it had appeared to pursue a policy of equal friendship with both the PRC and the USSR. After 1958, that is after the PRC and the USSR fell out with each other, it joined in the polemics that raged between them. Evidently there was a great debate in the MPRP hierarchy concerning preference for Mongolia's ties with the PRC and the USSR. Yumzhagiin Tsedenbal, and his associates favoured close ties with the Soviet Union. Mongolia firmly supported the USSR in the latter's rift with Albania, which first came to light at the Twenty-second Congress of the CPSU held in Moscow from 17 to 31 October 1961. It echoed Soviet reactions to the Hungarian and Czechoslovak revolts and the problem of Yugoslavia. It fully supported the Soviet stand on Asian and international issues. In other words, the independent Mongolian stance between the PRC and the USSR had gone.

When the People's Liberation Army (PLA) of China began its march from Manchuria to the south in February 1949, Mao sought Stalin's opinion concerning Mongolia joining China. Stalin answered that, in the Soviet opinion, Mongolia would not give up its independence for autonomy within China even if all Mongol lands formed a single autonomous entity, and that it was up to Mongolia to decide on this.

On the occasion of the fifth anniversary celebrations of the PRC, the Chinese leaders (Mao Zedong, Zhou Enlai and their associates) raised the question of the liquidation of the independence of Mongolia and its return to China with the Soviet leaders (N.S. Khrushchev, N.A. Bulganin and their associates), who were then in China to attend the celebrations. According to the Soviets, the Soviet leaders refused to discuss the matter, stating that Mongolia belonged to the Mongols and its destiny had to be decided in Ulan Bator and not in Beijing or Moscow.

After the Twentieth Congress of the CPSU in 1956, the Chinese leaders attempted to use its criticism of Stalin's personality cult to further their own interests. While commending the Soviet leaders for their criticism of the cult of personality and for their resolve to end its negative consequences, they mentioned Stalin's refusal to allow the return of Mongolia to China and demanded correction of this mistake by the return of Mongolia to China. The Soviet leaders declared that Mongolia was an independent country and had not formed part of China since 1921.

As Marxists themselves, the Chinese leaders understood well the language of the Soviet leaders on both the occasions. Nevertheless on 10 July 1964 Mao Zedong said to a Japanese journalist in Beijing:

> In accordance with the Yalta agreement, the Soviet Union, under the pretext of guaranteeing the independence of Mongolia, actually

placed that country under its domination ... In 1954, when Khrushchev and Bulganin arrived in Cuba, we raised the question, but they refused to talk with us.

Obviously, the result of the plebiscite held on 20 October 1945, which Mao had accepted in Moscow on 14 February 1950, and the rebuff of Khrushchev to him and his associates to discuss Mongolia's status in 1954 and 1956 had not settled the question.

The first large-scale departure of Chinese labourers from Mongolis occured in May 1962. The Cultural Revolution of China (1967-76), however, marked the lowest ebb in the relations between China and Mongolia. China recalled its ambassodor from Ulan Bator, and Mongolia withdrew its from Beijing. On grounds of internal security the MPR expelled several Chinese embassy personnel and teachers from Ulan Bator. Consequent to several border incidents, China and Mongolia closed their common border and cut off the Beijing-Ulan Bator railway link.

Mongolia aud the Soviet Union concluded several agreements on economic and technical aid. An agreement signed by Nikita Khrushchev and Yumzhagiin Tsedenbal in Moscow on 19 February 1959 specially provided for Soviet assistance in the reclamation of large areas of virgin lands in Mongolia. Mongolia also joined the Council for Mutual Economic Assistance (CMEA), a device for integrating the economies of the Socialist countries more closely with the economy of the Sovit Union, of the Warsaw Pact countries on 7 June 1962. It had sent observers to CMEA meetings from 1958 to 1962. It was the first Asian country to join the CMEA.

Mongolia and the Soviet Union signed a 20-year Treaty of Friendship, Cooperation and Mutual Assistance in Ulan Bator on 15 January 1966. A Soviet Government and Party delegation headed by Leonid Ilyich Brezhnev concluded the treaty. Breshnev, who signed the treaty on behalf of the Soviet Union, said:

> As is known, [the People's Republic of] China has not renounced its claims towards its northern neighbours, and this is sufficient for both the Soviet Union and Mongolia to be vigilant ... [The] basic sense of the Soviet-Mongolian treaty lies in the fact that it recognizes the real possibility that the independence of a socialist country can be endangered by another socialist country.

The treaty strengthened Mongolian-Soviet ties. It guaranteed their defence, security, independence and territorial integrity in the event of interference by any third country. Briefly, the treaty of 1966 renewed the arrangements first made under the Mongolian-Soviet treaty of 1946.

Apparently, the Soviet-Mongolian treaty of 1966 was not favourable to Chinese interests in Mongolia. Soviet-Mongolian treaties in the past had been directed first against the threat of aggression from Japan and secondly against the Republic of China. Not only did the 1966 treaty aim at preventing and eliminatihg the threat of aggression from the PRC, but it also underlined the importance of the aim of Soviet-Mongolian cooperation.

The Soviet Government introduced its military units in Mongolia in the spring of 1966. These units could play a defensive as well as an offensive role along its eastern flank. Within the framework of the Soviet-Mongolian treaty of 1966 they are now under the joint command headquarters at Chita, first established in the spring of 1982, for the three military districts of Siberia, Transbaikal (extending up to the Pacific Ocean) and the Far East. The estimated strength of these Soivet units in Mongolia is 50,000 troops.

The Mongolian-Chinese frontier is strategically most sensitive although its importance in other respects, for example economically, is not very great. North-western Manchuria, Inner Mongolia and Northeastern Xinjiang are highly vulnerable to powerful Soviet strike forces.

None the less the Soviet Union and Mongolia continued to support the PRC in certain respects. Said the joint Mongolian-Soviet communique of 15 January 1966:

> The sides [i.e. the MPR and the USSR] reiterate their support for the joint struggle of the Chinese people to liberate Taiwan, which is an inalienable part of the People's Republic of China. They repeat their demand that the Chiang Kai-shek clique should be expelled from the United Nations and the legitimate rights of the People's Republic of China be restored in the Organization.[3]

On 2 September 1968, on the occasion of the anniversary of defeat of Japan at the hands of the USSR and the MPR, the USSR warned the PRC that an attack on Mongolia would be dealt with in the same way that the Japanese threat had been dealt with in the 1930s, i.e. with military force.

The PRC had long accused the USSR of trying to control the

MPR. It now characterized Mongolia as a Soviet colony. This outraged Mongolian sentiment. Said the Mongolian newspaper *Unen* (Ulan Bator): "Enraged by the fact that Mao's dream of seeing Mongolia as part of China does not come true, the Beijing clique seeks to drive a wedge into the traditional fraternal relations between our country and the Soviet Union." It added: "The word colony reminds us of the dark times when we were languishing for 220 years under the yoke of Manchu Chinese colonialists, who ruthlessly pillaged our country, kept it in mediaeval ignorance and brutally exploited our people, taking them to the brink of extinction as a nation".

The restoration of ambassadorial-level relations between the two countries in 1971 raised the possibility of normalization of their mutual relations. But discussions between Beijing and Ulan Bator resulted only in the transfer of the last uncompleted buildings of the unfinished Chinese projects to Mongolian hands in May 1973. Political relations between Beijing and Ulan Bator remained still sour.

Zhou Enlai asked for the withdrawal of Soviet forces from Mongolia at the Tenth Congress of the Communist Party of China (CPC) held in Beijing between 24 and 28 August 1973. Ever Since the PRC had not ceased to demand the withdrawal of Soviet forces from Mongolia, because it feels that Soviet forces in Mongolia threaten its security. The MPR, which considers this an interference in its internal affairs, says that Soviet troops in Mongolia are under the Mongolian-Soviet treaty of 1966 and that these troops had come to Mongolia at its specific request at a time when the Chinese leaders were making military preparations along the Mongolian-Chinese borders.

Following his meeting with President Gerald Ford of the United States in Vladivostok, President Leonid Brezhnev visited Ulan Bator on 26 November. On that occasion he and Yumzhagiin Tsedenbal made their assessment of China. Brezhnev emphasized Soviet-Mongolian friendship and cooperation and criticized China for its claim to Soviet territory. Tsedenbal described China as chauvinistic and expressed "resolute opposition to the expansionist policy of China in regard to the sovereign independent socialist Mongolian State".

Sinch 1936 Mao's stance towards Mongolia always was that Mongolia should become part of China. Even after the establishment of diplomatic relations between the PRC and the MPR, he did not give up claim to Mongolia. Mao's successors adhere to his pronouncements concerning the status of Mongolia. Cainese historians interpret the Mongolian Revolution of 1921 as the struggle of the people of Mongolia, a country forming part of China, against aggression from Russia.

On 12 April 1978 Ulan Bator sent the following note to Beijing:

> If the Chinese leadership renounces for ever its policy of annexation in regard to the MPR and embarks on the road of good-neighbourliness and co-operation with the MPR and USSR, the existing need for the presence in the MPR of Soviet military units will no longer be there. When and how soon this is going to take place depends on the Chinese side.

There is no evidence or indication if Beijing ever replied to this note from the Mongolian Government.

The answer of Yumzhaggin Tsedenbal to a question raised by a correspondent of the British Broadcasting Corporation (BBC) concerning the Mongolian-Chinese relations in July 1981 is an interesting exposition of the MPR's China policy and attitude. It bears full reproduction :

> After the victory of the people's revolution in China our Government officially recognized the People's Republic of China, and diplomatic relations were established between the two countries. Today our states continue to maintain diplomatic relations. Unfortunately, it cannot be said that Mongolian-Chinese relations are normal at present. The reason lies in the policy of China's ruling circles, directed against the freedom and independence of the Mongolian People's Republic.
>
> The Chinese rulers are trying to spread the impression everywhere in the world that the MPR is Chinese territory which is to be "seized". A secondary school textbook put out in 1978 describes the whole of Mongolia as an integral part of China. Moreover, part of the territory of the Soviet Union is also shown as belonging to China. In this connection the dangerous character of the policy pursued by the Chinese leaders poisoning the minds of China's younger generation with the idea of annexation of foreign territories should be emphasized.
>
> In an attempt to substantiate the expansionist policy *vis-a-vis* the MPR, the Beijing rulers shamelessly distort objective historical facts. They vainly seek to prove that from ancient times Mongolia was part of China. The Chinese ruling circles acclaim the aggres-

sive wars waged by the Mongol khans in the Middle Ages to justify their claims to the territories of other countries.

The Beijing leaders are guided by expansionist aims as regards our country. They are engaged in war preparations, concentrating their troops near our border and building military strategic installations. The bulk of China's armed forces had been spearheaded against the USSR and the MPR. We have, therefore, long been compelled to spend considerable funds, which could have been channelled for peaceful construction, and allocate them for defence purposes. Safeguarding freedom and independence, the MPR relies on Soviet aid through the Treaty of Friendship, Cooperation and Mutual Assistance concluded between the MPR and the USSR in 1966. In conformity with this treaty and on the basis of a request voiced by our Government, a certain contingent of Soviet troops is stationed on Mongolian territory, which together with the Mongolian Armed Forces, is safeguarding freedom and independence of our people.

The Chinese side regularly sends its agents to our country to carry out subversive activity. For the same purpose it is trying to use Chinese emissaries (*huaqiao*) residing in Mongolia.

The MPR pursued, and continues to pursue, a principled policy *vis-a-vis* the PRC. We adhere to our line of normalizing relations with China on the basis of the principle of peaceful co-existence. We have stated this fact on a number of occasions. The normalization of relations beween China and our country depends on whether the Chinese leaders abandon their expansionist line and the practice of Maoism.

The PRC's ruling circles are following the policy of great power hegemonism in respect of other neighbouring countries as well. This fact is well known to the world public. In collusion with the USA, the Chinese leaders are waging an undeclared war against the Democratic Republic of Afghanistan. They accomplished an overt armed aggression against Vietnam and continue to encroach on its independence and territorial integrity. Beijing supports and arms the remnants of the Pol Pot regime and organizes armed aggression against the People's Republic of Kampuchea. It is also engaged in hostile intrigues against the Lao People's Democratic Republic. It conducts subversive activities directed at destabilizing the situation in India. The Chinese rulers enter into collusion with most reactionary forces in their aggressive actions against the security, independence and social progress of the peoples.

In January 1982, the Mongolian Government expelled many ethnic Chinese living in Ulan Bator for certain crimes like smuggling and resettled them in the Selenga Valley in the northern part of the country. From 9 March to 1 June 1983, it ordered nearly 2,000 ethnic Chinese living in Ulan Bator to leave for state farms in the rural areas or face expulsion. Beijing protested against these orders. Ulan Bator rejected the protest, but hoped that Beijing could ask its nationals in Mongolia to do nothing which might impede improvement of the Mongolian-Chinese relations. There are nearly 10,000 Chinese nationals in Mongolia today, most of them living in Ulan Bator. Till the establishment of revolutionary Mongolia in the 1920s, especially the establishment of the MPR in 1924, the Chinese dominated the non-livestock aspects of Mongolian life and economy. They did all kinds of work that the Mongols themselves did not like to do. They included carpenters, smiths, tailors, barbers, shoemakers, household servants and others. Most of them had left Mongolia by the 1930s. The ethnic Chinese now resident in Ulan Bator were part of the group of labourers who first came to Mongolia under the Chinese-Mongolian agreement of 1952 and who stayed on even after the expiry of that agreement in the 1970s. One clause of the agreement of 1952 provided that any Chinese had the option of taking the citizenship of the MPR.

Border incidents and illegal movement of border markers had also strained relations between China and Mongolia for 20 years. However, Chinese-Mongolian relations have shown signs of definite improvement in recent years. In April 1984 Beijing disclosed that the Chinese-Mongolian border commission had met for six months as stipulated in the boundary treaty of 1962. On 19 July 1984 the Governments of the PRC and the MPR signed in Beijing a protocol on the joint surveillance of their common borders. On 9 August 1986 Mongolia and China signed a consular treaty in Ulan Bator.[4] All this perhaps indicated an improvement in relations not only between the two countries, but also between the PRC and the USSR. Of course, the nature of Chinese-Mongolian relationship will ultimately be determined by the nature of Chinese-Soviet relationship.

The PRC, however, continues to demand the withdrawal of Soviet troops from Mongolia as a pre-condition for the normalization of its relations with the USSR. The Soviets say that the Chinese demand involves third parties. On 2 March 1984 President Konstantin Chernenko said that the Soviet Union could make no agreement with

China that would harm the interests of other states. The Mongols do not of course pay heed to the Chinese demand for the withdrawal of Soviet troops from their country. On the other hand, they talk of Chinese military build-up along the Mongolian-Chinese borders.

The attitude of Mongolia towards China today is thus the result of a lingering suspicion among the leaders of Mongolia that the old Chinese conception of Mongolia as part of China may not have really disappeared even after the establishment of communist power in China.

Mongolia condemns China's attitude towards Afghanistan and Vietnam, not because of the fraternal solidarity with the USSR or the closeness of its foreign policy to that of the USSR, but because of China's tendency to treat its neighbours as "lost" Chinese territories. Thus, there is more in the MPR's criticism of the PRC's policies towards Afghanistan and Vietnam for independence and sovereignty.

Thus the main factors determining the alliance between Mongolia and the Soviet Union are the Mongol uneasiness about the intentions of China towards their country, that is, their fear of annexation by China. Pro-Sovietism, therefore, is a deliberate decision of the Mongols. It marks a switch in Mongolian policy away from China and, as such, constitutes the most important development in Mongolia's relations with China and Russia since the convention of Mongol nobles held at Dolonnor/Miao on 29 May—3 June 1691.

China and Mongolia are adjacent countries, but they are distant neighbours. Once dominant, China has had no influence in Mongolia since the 1920s. The Chinese leaders refuse, as always, to renounce their claims to Mongolia. Even with the passing away of Mao Zedong, the "great helmsman". there is no change in the PRC's policy towards Mongolia. Normalization of relations between China and the Soviet Union may facilitate normalization of relations between China and Mongolia. Only time will tell.

Mongolia and the Soviet Union are neighbours. The two countries have one ideology, one aim. They have extremely close relations. Mongolia's close association with the Soviet Union is so evident from its foreign policy of cosistently following the Soviet lead in international relations. On 12 November 1973 Tsedenbal stated Mongolia's relationship with the Soviet Union and other Socialist countries :

> Proceeding from the fact that the MPR's successful advance along the road of building a socialist society is possible on the basis of the utmost strengthening of the traditional friendship and close

cooperation with our loyal friend the Soviet Union and other countries of the socialist community, our Party consistently pursues a course in its foreign policy aimed at further deepening and broadening the fraternal friendship and multifacted cooperation with all the fraternal countries and their Marxist-Leninist parties.[5]

Thus the main objective of Mongolia's policy is to consolidate alliance and close co-operation with the Soviet Union and other Socialist countries.

The Soviet Union also encourages direct contacts between Mongolia and its own Buryat and Tuvan autonomous republics as well as between Mongolia and the Soviet Central Asian republics. Soviet influence in Mongolia thus covers all aspects of Mongolian life—cultural, economic and political.

Of course Mongolia retains its strategic importance between China and the USSR. A fact of geography, namely that China and the USSR have a frontier with Mongolia to defend, and a fact of politics, namely that they have no one to defend it for them—these were the origins of the game in Mongolia. Even today the game is the same, but what a difference in the way it is played : Apparently, China has lost the game in Mongolia, but has it really ?

NOTES AND REFERENCES

1. Communist Party of Mongolia.
2. Beijing 10 August 1962.
3. *Unen*, Ulan Bator, 15 March 1966.
4. The duties and functions of consular officials are different from those of diplomatic officials.
5. MONTSAME (Mongolian Telegraph Agency), Ulan Bator, 12 November 1973.

POSTFACE

I began this study by saying that Afghanistan and Mongolia are independent sovereign states and members of the United Nations. I end it by saying that Afghanistan and Mongolia, although members of the United Nations, are now dependencies of the USSR. They are now so close to the USSR that they have even abandoned their independent foreign policies. Afghanistan, Mongolia and the Soviet Union now have common interests and common foriegn policies. As small states, Afghanistan and Mongolia cannot have their own foriegn policies.

If the Soviet Union has not absorbed Afghanistan and Mongolia into its political framework, it is because it is just not in the Soviet interest to do so. It is in the Soviet interest that both Afghanistan and Mongolia maintain all the formal features of independence under its tutelage. The question facing Afghanistan and Mongolia now is not one of independence from the USSR, but one of dependence on it, for both seem to be open to violation from their neighbours. And they may not by themselves be able to defend themselves and preserve whatever independence they possess without Soviet military assistance. Dependence on the Soviet Union, therefore, is a geopolitical necessity of Afghanistan and Mongolia.

Mikhail Gorbachev's declaration in Vladivostok on 28 July 1986 to withdraw certain number of Soviet forces from Afghanistan and Mongolia in order to improve relations with the neighbouring countries shows that the Soviet military position in the two countries is so sound that partial withdrawal of Soviet troops from there would not impair that position and/or security in any way. In any event Moscow will not do anything which may jeoperdize its position there.

With Afghanistan and Mongolia within its influence, the USSR has, along its southern flank as along its western flank, a chain of land-locked, friendly and allied states to insulate and secure it from external aggression. Xinjiang, China's westermost region, remains the only gap.

Xinjiang borders the USSR along a line over a thousand miles long. It has held importance for it ever since the mid-nineteenth century, when Russian troops first clashed with Chinese pickets on what is now the Chinese-Soviet border in Central Asia. There was much trouble over the question of border trade and other similar matters between China and Russia from 1854 to 1857. At certain times especially during the Russian occupation of the Ili from 1871 to 1881 and after, Russian influence in Xinjiang (then Sinkiang) was, indeed, paramount.

The Soviets intervened in Xinjiang early in 1933. They did so probably because of the fear that the Japanese might drive through Xinjiang from northwest China and invade its part of Central Asia. An agreement, signed on 1 February 1936, developed the closest political ties between the USSR and Xinjiang. In 1944 the Soviets conrrolled the non-Han, mainly Kazak, uprising in the East Turkistan Republic comprising the three districts of Altai, Ili and Tarbagatai. After the Chinese-Soviet Treaty of Friendship, Alliance and Mutual Assistance of 1950, the most important agreement that the Soviet Government signed with the Chinese Government in Beijing on 12 October 1954 related to the construction of railway lines linking the PRC and the USSR through Xinjiang. The misunderstanding and eventual conflict between the PRC and the USSR during 1959-69 perhaps ended all Soviet amibtions in Xinjiang But did it really ?

How Xinjiang escaped Tsarist/Soviet annexation or did not become a buffer between China and Russia/USSR is interesting. Perhaps, with Xinjiang becoming a province and hence an integral part of China in 1884, Russia (later the Soviet Union) felt constrained (owing to its own policy of respecting the territorial integrity of China) to alter its status. Anyway a strong China will never allow the Soviet Union to stage a comeback there. And China is strong today, although not as strong as the Soviet Union. Even then, who knows what may happen in Xinjiang ? Because, in spite of Moscow's control of Afghanistan and Mongolia or the Soviet Union's special relationship with them, the centuries-old struggle for mastery over Central Asia is not yet over. Whether an adjacent area or nation can forcibly be taken into or kept within the People's Republic of China or the USSR is a moot point. But then which nation has not done so. Historically Moscow always considered annexing an adjacent territory as the most expedient means of securing its frontiers. In Russian eyes territorial expansion was always a "defensive expansion" inspired

Postface

by the lack of defensive frontiers and by the harsh experience of past generations in which invading Russia had been an endemic habit of powerful European nations and Asian tribes. How is it in Soviet eyes ?

My study also shows that, as always, both Afghanistan and Mongolia continue to retain as ever their importance in regional and international politics by virtue of their geography—their location—between China, India, Iran and the USSR. Of course, Afghanistan is more important than Mongolia. Afghanistan is of concern to China, Pakistan, Iran, the USSR and others, Mongolia is of concern to China and the USSR only. Afghanistan is close to crisis zones like the Indian Ocean. Mongolia is rather remote from crisis zones like the Pacific Ocean.

APPENDIXES

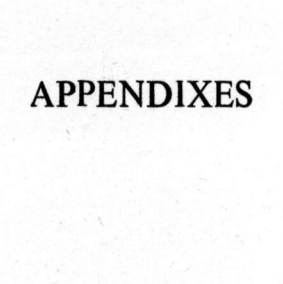

APPENDIX I

AFGHANISTAN USSR
TREATY OF FRIENDSHIP, 1921

With a view to strengthening friendly relations between Russia and Afghanistan and confirming the actual independence of Afghanistan, the Russian Soviet Federated Socialist Republic of the one part and the sovereign state of Afghanistan of the other part have decided to conclude the present Treaty, for which purpose there have been appointed as their plenipotentiaries:

For the Government of the Russian Soviet Federated Socialist Republic:

Georgi Vasilievich Chicherin
Lyov Mikhailovich Karakhan

For the Government of the sovereign state of Afghanistan:

Muhammad Wali Khan
Mirza Muhammad Khan
Ghulam Sadiq Khan

The above named plenipotentiaries, after mutual presentation of their credentials, which were found to be in due and proper form, have agreed as follows:

ARTICLE 1
The High Contracting Parties, recognizing their mutual independence and binding themselves to respect it, now mutually enter into regular diplomatic relations.

ARTICLE 2
The High Contracting Parties bind themselves not to enter into any military or political agreement with a third party which may prejudice one of the Contracting Parties.

ARTICLE 3
The legations and consulates of the High Contracting Parties shall mutually and equally enjoy diplomatic privileges in accordance with the uses of International Law.

Note I
There shall be included in that category-
(*a*) The right to hoist the state flag.
(*b*) Personal inviolability of registered members of legation and consulates.
(*c*) Inviolability of diplomatic correspondence and of persons fulfilling the duties of couriers with every kind of mutual assistance in these matters.
(*d*) Communication by telephone, wireless and telegraph in accordance with the privileges of diplomatic representatives.
(*e*) Extraterritoriality of premises occupied by Legations and consulates, but without the right of giving asylum to persons who are officially recognized by their local government as having broken the laws of the country.

Note II
The military attaches of both Contracting Parties shall be attached to their legations on the basis of equality as regards the above.

ARTICLE 4
The High Contracting parties mutually agree to the opening of five consulates of the Russian Soviet Federated Socialist Republic on Afghan territory and of seven consulates of Afghanistan on Russian territory, of which five shall be within the boundaries of Russian Central Asia.

In addition to the above, the opening of further consulates and consular posts in Russia and Afghanistan shall be arranged in each particular case by special agreement between the High Contracting Parties.

ARTICLE 5
Russian consulates shall be established at Herat, Meimen, Mazar-i-Sharif, Kandahar and Ghazni. Afghan consulates shall be established as follows: a consulate-general at Tashkent and consulates at Petrograd, Kazan, Samarkand, Merv and Krasnovodsk.

The manner and time of the actual opening of the Russian consu-

Appendix

lates in Afghanistan and of the Afghan consulates in Russia shall be defined by special agreement between the two Contracting Parties.

ARTICLE 6
Russia agrees to the free and untaxed transit through its territory of all kinds of goods purchased by Afghanistan either in Russia itself, through state organizations, or from abroad.

ARTICLE 7
The High Contracting Parties recognize and accept the freedom of Eastern nations on the basis of independence and in accordance with the general wish of each nation.

ARTICLE 8
In confirmation of Article 7 of the present Treaty, the High Contracting Parties accept the actual independance and freedom of Bukhara and Khiva, whatever may be the form of their government, in accordance with the wishes of their peoples.

ARTICLE 9
In fulfilment of and in accordance with the promise of the Russian Soviet Federated Socialist Republic, expressed by Lenin as its head to the Minister Plenipotentiary of the sovereign state of Afghanistan, Russia agrees to hand over to Afghanistan the frontier districts which belonged to the latter in the last century, observing the principles of justice and self-determination of the population inhabiting the same. The manner in which such self-determiation and will of the majority of the regular local population shall be expressed shall be settled by a special treaty between the two states through the intermediary of plenipotentiaries of both parties.

ARTICLE 10
In order to strengthen friendly relations between the High Contracting Parties, the Government of the Russian Soviet Federated Socialist Republic agrees to give to Afghanistan financial and other assistance.

ARTICLE 11
The present Treaty is drawn up in the Russian and Persian languages; both texts are accounted authentic.

ARTICLE 12

The present Treaty shall come into force upon its ratification by the governments of the High Contracting Parties. The exchange of ratifications shall take place at Kabul, in witness whereof the plenipotentiaries of both parties have signed the present Treaty and set their seals thereto.

Moscow, 28 February 1921.

AFGHANISTAN-USSR TREATY OF PEACE, GOOD NEIGHBOURLINESS AND COOPERATION, 1978

The Union of Soviet Socialist Republics and the Democratic Republic of Afghanistan

Reaffirming their commitment to the aims and principles of the Soviet-Afghan treaties of 1921 and 1931, which laid the basis for friendly and good neighbourly relations between the Soviet and Afghan peoples and which meet their basic national interests

Willing to strengthen in every way friendship and all round cooperation between the two countries

Being determined to develop social and economic achievements of the Soviet and Afghan peoples, to safeguard their security and independence, to come out resolutely for the cohesion of all the forces fighting for peace, national independence, democracy and social progress

Expressing their firm detemination to facilitate the strengthening of peace and security in Asia and the whole world, to make their contribution towards developing relations among states and strengthening fruitful and mutually beneficial co-operation in Asia, attaching great importance to the further consolidation of the contractual-legal basis of their relations

Reaffirming their dedication to the aims and principles of the United Nations Charter

Decided to conclude the present Treaty of Friendship, Good Neighbourliness and Co-operation and agreed on the following :

ARTICLE 1

The High Contracting Parties solemnly declare their determination to strengthen and deepen the inviolable friendship between the two countries and to develop all round co-operation on the basis of equality, respect for national sovereignty, territorial integrity and non-interference in each other's internal affairs.

ARTICEE 2

The High Contracting Parties shall make efforts to strengthen and broaden mutually beneficial economic, scientific and technical co-operation between them. With these aims in view, they shall develop and deepen co-operation in the fields of industry, transport, communications, agriculture, the use of natural resources, development of the powergenerating industry and other branches of economy to give each other assistance in the training of national personnel and in planning the development of the national economy. The two sides shall expand trade on the basis of the principles of equality, mutual benefit and most-favoured nation treatment.

ARTICLE 3

The High Contracting Parties shall promote the development of co-operation and exchange of experience in the fields of science, culture, art, literature, enducation, health services, the press, radio, television, cinema, tourism, sport and other fields.

The two sides shall facilitate the expansion of co-operation between organs of state power and public organizations, enterprises, cultural and scientific institutions with a view to making a deeper acquaintance of the life, work experience and achivements of the peoples of the two countries.

ARTICLE 4

The High Contracting Parties, acting in the spirit of the traditions of friendship and good neighbourliness as well as the United Nations Charter, shall consult each other and take by agreement appropriate measures to ensure the security, independence and teritorial integrity of the two countries.

In the interests of strengthening the defence capacity of the High Contracting Parties they shall continue to develop co-operation in the military field on the basis of appropriate agreements concluded between them.

ARTICLE 5

The Union of Soviet Socialist Republics respects the policy of non-aligrment wnich is pursued by the Democratic Republic of Afghanistan and which is an important factor for maintaining international peace and security.

The Democratic Republic of Afghanistan respects the policy of peace pursued by the Union of Soviet Socialist Republics and aimed at strengthening friendship and co-operation with all countries and peoples

ARTICLE 6
Each of the High Contracting Parties solemnly declares that it shall not join any military or other alliances or take part in any groupings of states as well as in actions or measures directed against the other High Contracting Party.

ARTICLE 7
The High Contracting Parties shall continue to make every effort to defend international peace and the security of the peoples, to deepen the process of relaxation of international tension, to spread it to all areas of the world, including Asia, to translate it into concrete forms of mutually beneficial co-operation among states and to settle international disputed issues by peaceful means.

The two sides ahall actively contribute towards general and complete disarmament, including nuclear disarmament, under effective international control.

ARTICLE 8
The High Contracting Parties shall facilitate development of co-operation among Asian states and the establishment of relations of peace, good neighbourliness and mutual confidence among them and the creation of an effective security system in Asia on the basis of joint efforts by all countries of the continent.

ARTICLE 9
The High Contracting Parties shall continue their consistent struggle against machinations by the forces of aggression, for the final elimination of colonialism and racism in all their forms and manifestations.

The two sides shall co-operate with each other and with other peace loving states in supporting the just struggle of the peoples for their freedom, independence, sovereignty and social progress.

ARTICLE 10
The High Contracting Parties shall consult each other on all major international issues affecting the interests of the two countries.

Appendix

ARTICLE 11
The High Contracting Parties state that their commitments under the existing international treaties do not contradict the provisions of the present Treaty and undertake not to conclude any international agreements incompatible with it.

ARTICLE 12
Questions, which may arise between the High Contracting Parties concerning the interpretation or application of any provision of the present Treaty, shall be settled bilaterally in the spirit of friendship, mutual understanding and respect.

ARTICLE 13
The present Treaty shall remain in force within twenty years of the day it becomes effective.

Unless one of the High Contracting Parties declares six months before the expiration of this term of its desire to terminate the Treaty, it shall remain in force for the next five years until one of the High Contracting Parties warns in writing the other Party, six months before the expiration of current five-year term, about its intention to terminate the Treaty.

ARTICLE 14
If one of the High Contracting Parties expresses the wish in the course of the twenty-year term of the Treaty to terminate it before its expiration date, it shall notify in writing the other Party, six months before the suggested date of expiration of the Treaty, about its desire to terminate the Treaty before the expiration of the term and may consider the Treaty terminated as of the date thus set.

ARTICLE 15
The present Treaty shall be ratified and take effect on the day of exchange of the instruments of ratification, which is to take place in Kabul.

Done in two copies, each in the Russian and Dari languages, both texts being equally authentic.

Moscow, 4 December 1978.

APPENDIX II

MONGOLIA-USSR FRIENDSHIP PACT, 1921

ARTICLE 1
The Russian Soviet and the Revolutionary Mongol Governments mutually recognize each other as the only governments in the territory of Russia and Mongolia.

ARTICLE 2
Both Governments agree mutually to respect each other, and not to allow on their territory the formation of groups, or the recruiting of troops, hostile to one of the Contracting Parties, as also not to allow the transportation of arms and the transit of troops, hostile to one of the Contracting Parties, through their territory.

ARTICLE 3
Both Government will establish, at their discretion, consulates in necessary places.

ARTICLE 4
The question of frontier delimitation must be decided immediately by a mixed Russo-Mongol commission.

ARTICLE 5
The citizens of Russia and Mongolia, residing on the territory of the other Contracting Party, must be judged, both in civil and in criminal cases, according to the laws of their own country.

ARTICLE 6
Taxes on imports and exports will also be fixed by a mixed commission.

ARTICLE 7
The Soviet Government undertakes to establish in Mongolia, free of charge, postal and telegraphic communications, and will supply

the necssary materials for this purpose, whereupon a special postal and telegraphic convention will be signed.

ARTICLE 8
The Mongolian Government recognizes the right of property on land within its territory, and agrees to give the ground-space necessary for buildings of diverse kinds, and for railways built with Russian capital.

ARTICLE 9
The present Pact comes into force from the day of the signature by the representatives of the Contracting Parties.

Moscow, 5 November 1921.

MPR-USSR TREATY OF FRIENDSHIP, COOPERATION AND MUTUAL ASSISTANCE, 1966

The Presidium of the Supreme Soviet of the Union of Soviet Socialist Republics and the Presidium of the Great People's Khural of the Mongolian People's Republic

Reaffirming the loyalty of the Soviet and Mongolian peoples to the purposes and principles of the Treaty of Friendship and Mutual Assistance between the Union of Soviet Socialist Republics and the Mongolian People's Republic and the Agreement on economic and cultural co-opration between the Government of the Union of Soviet Socialist Republics and the Government of the Mongolian People's Republic of 27 February 1946.

Expressing the sincere desire of the peoples of both countries to intensify and strengthen further the traditional unshakable friendship and the relations of all round close co-operation and fraternal mutual assistance between the Union of Soviet Socialist Republics and the Mongolian People's Republic on the basis of the principles of socialist internationalism.

Finally convinced that the development of relations between the two countries in this manner is in accordance with the vital interests of the Soviet and Mongolian peoples and with the interests of the socialist community.

Resolved to further in every possible way the preservation and consolidation of the peace and security of peoples in Asia and throughout the world.

Considering that the Treaty of Friendship and Mutual Assistance and the Agreement on economic and cultural co-operation of 27

February 1946, which have played an historic role in the steady development of relations of eternal friendship and fraternal co-operation between the two countries, are approaching the expiry of their terms and are in need of renewal in the light of the wealth of experience gained in the development of political, economic and cultural relations between the Union of Soviet Sociolist Republics and the Mongolian people's Republic and the changes which have taken place in Asia and throughout the world.

Have decided to conclude this Treaty and for that purpose have appointed as their plenipotentiaries :

The Presidium of the Supreme Soviet of the Union of Soviet Socialist Republics: Leonid Ilyich Brezhnev

The Presidium of the Great People's Khural of the Mongolian People's Republic: Yumzhagiin Tsedenbal

Who, having exchanged their full powers, fuond in due and good form, have agreed on the following :

ARTICLE 1

The high Coniracting Parties shall continue to strengthen the unshakable traditional friendship of the peoples of the Union of Soviet Socialist Republics and the Mongolian People's Republic and to develop all round co-opration and fraternal mutual assistance between the two countries on the basis of the principles of socialist internationalism.

ARTICLE 2

The High Contracting Parties shall continue to develop and intensify economic, scientific and technical co-operation between the two countries in accordance with the principles of friendly mutual assistance and mutual benefit both on a bilateral basis and within the framework of the multilateral co-operation of the socialist countries, including the Council for Mutual Economic Assistance.

ARTICLE 3

The High Contracting Parties shall steadily develop the cultural ties between the two countries through the further expansion of co-operation in the spheres of education, health, science, literature, art, the press, radio and television and physical culture and sports.

ARTICLE 4

On the basis of and pursuant to this Treaty, separate treaties and agreements shall be concluded between the Governmants and between the appropriate institutions and organizations of the two Parties.

Appendix

ARTICLE 5
The High Cantracting Parties shall assist each other in ensuring the defensive capacity of the two countries in accordance with the tasks involved in steadily strengthening the defensive power of the socia list community. The High Contracting Parties shall consult together on all major international problems affecting the interests of the two countries or the interests of peace and international co-operation and, acting in the spirit of their finest traditions and of the Charter of the United Nations, they shall jointly take all necessary measures, including military measures, with a view to ensuring the security, independence and territorial integrity of the two countries.

ARTICLE 6
The High Contracting Parties shall continue their efforts aimed at the preservation and strengthening of international peace and security of peoples, at the achievement of general and complete disarmament and at the complete elimination of colonialism in all its forms and manifestations. The High Contracting Parties confirm their readiness to participate, in a spirit of sincere co-oparation, in all international action designed to achieve these lofty aims.

ARTICLE 7
The High Contracting Parties shall consistently pursue a policy of maintaining and strenthening friendly relations and co-operation among states in Asia and shall act jointly to prevent and remove any threat of imperialist aggression in that part of the world.

ARTICLE 8
This Treaty shall not affect obligations assumed by the Parties under existing bilateral and multilateral agreements.

ARTICLE 9
This Treaty is subject to ratification and shall enter into force on the date of the exchange of the instruments of ratification, which shall take place in Moscow as soon as possible.

ARTICLE 10
This Treaty is concluded for a term of twenty years and shall be automatically extended for successive ten-year terms if neither of the High Contracting Parties gives notice of its desire to terminate it twelve months before the expiry of the current term.

Done at Ulan Bator on 15 January 1966 in duplicate in the Russian and Mongolian languages, both texts being equally authentic.

BIBLIOGRAPHY

Abdul Ghani, *A Review of the Political Situation in Central Asia*, Lahore, 1921.
Beddeley, J.P. *Russia, Mongolia, China*. 2 vols., London, 1919; reprint New York, 1969.
Clubb. O. Edmund, *China and and Russia*: *"The Great Game"*, New York, 1971.
Dallin, David J., *The Rise of Russia in Asia*, New Haven, 1949; reprint 1971.
Ingram, Edward, *The Beginning of the Great Game in Asia 1828-1834*, London, 1979.
Jukes, Geoffrey, *The Soviet Union in Asia*, Sydney, 1973.
Krause Alexis, *Russia in Asia, 1558-1899*, New York, 1899.
Kuno; Yoshi S. *Japanese Expansion on the Asiatic Continent*, 2 vols., Berkeley, 1937-40.
Phillips, G D.R., *Russia, Japan and Mongolia*, London, 1942.
Terentiev, M., *Russia and England in Central Asia*, 2 vols., Calcutta, 1876.

AFGHANISTAN

Adamec, Ludwig W., *Afghanistan 1900-1923: a diplomatic history*, Berkeley, 1967.
Akhramovich, R.T., *Outline History of Afghanistan After the Second World War*, Moscow, 1966.
Bilgrami, Ashgar H., *Afghanistan and British India, 1793-1907*, New Delhi, 1972.
Caroe, Olaf, *The Pathans 550 BC—AD 1957*, London, 1958.
Franck, Peter G., *Afghanistan Between East and West*, Washington, D.,C, 1956.
Fraser-Tytler, W.K., *Afghanistan: a study of political developments in Central Asia*, London, 1950.
Ganda Singh, *Ahmad Shah Durrani: Father of Modern Afghanistan* Bombay, 1959.

Gregorian, Vartan, *The Emergence of Modern Afghanistan: Politics of Reform and Modernization 1880-1946*, Stanford, 1969.
Giffitts, John C., *Afghanistan: Key to a Continent*, London, 1963.
Hammonds, Thomas T., *Red Flag Over Afghanistan*, Boulder, 1984.
Hyman, Anthony, *Afghanistan under Soviet Domination 1964-83*, London, 1984.
Khalfin, Naftula, *British Plots Against Afghanistan*, Moscow, 1981.
Khan, Sultan Mahomed, ed., *The Life of Abdur Rahman*, 2 vols., London, 1900.
Kohzad, Ahmad Ali, *Men and events through 18th and 19th Century Afghanistan*, Kabul, 1972.
Male, Beverley, *Revolutionary Afghanistan*. London & Canberra, 1982.
Mohammed Ali, *Afghanistan: The War of Independence 1919*. Kabul, 1960.
Newell, Richard. S., and Nancy S. Newell, *Struggle for Afghanistan*. Ithaca, N.Y., 1982.
Norris, J.A., *The First Afghan War 1838-1842*, Cambridge. 1967.
Poullada, Leon B., *Reform and Rebellion in Afghanistan 1919-1929*, Ithaca, N.Y., 1973.
Schinasi, May, *Afghanistan at the beginning of the Twentieth Century*, Naples, 1979.
Schofield, Victoria, *North-West Frontier and Afghanistan*, London, 1984.
Spain, James W., *The Pathan Borderland*, The Hague, 1963.
Stewort, Rhea Talley, *Years of Fire: Afghanistan 1914-1929*, New York, 1970.
Watson, Robert Grant, *History of Persia from the Beginning of the Nineteenth Century to the Year 1858*, London, 1866.
Wild, Roland, *Amanullah*, London, 1932.
Yapp, M.E., *Strategies of British India*, London, 1980.

MONGOLIA

Bawden, C.R., *The Modern History of Mongolia*, London, 1968.
Brown William A., and Urgunge Onon, *History of Mongolian People's Republic*, Cambridge, Mass., 1976; trans. from Mongolian.
Chapman, Walter, *Kublai Khan*, New York, 1966.
Coox, Alvin D., *Nomanhan: Japan Against Russia, 1939*, 2 vols., Stanford, 1986.
Dugersuren, M., *The Mongolian People's Republic and International Relations*, Ulan Bator, 1981.

Ewing, Thomas E., *Between the Hammer and the Anvil: Chinese and Russian Policies in Outer Mongolia 1911-1921*, Bloomington, In., 1980.
Friters, Gerald M., *Outer Mongolia and its International Position*, Baltimore, 1949.
Harrison, Marguerite, *Red Bear or Yellow Dragon*, London, 1924.
Larson, Frans August, *Duke of Mongolia*, Boston, 1930.
Ma Ho-t'ien, *Chinese Agent in Mongolia*, Baltimore, 1949.
Mancall, Mark, *Russia and China: Their Diplomatic Relations to 1728*, Cambridge, Mass., 1971.
Mishima Yasuo, and Tomio Goto, *A Japanese View of Outer Mongolia*, Tokyo, 1937.
Mongolian Academy of Sciences and USSR Academy of Sciences, *History of the Mongolian People's Republic* (in Mongolian and Russian), Ulan Bator and Moscow, 1954.
Murphy, George G.S., *Soviet Mongolia: a study of the oldest satellite*, Berkeley/Los Angeles, 1966.
"Nauka" Publishing House, *History of the Mongolian People's Republic*, Moscow, 1973.
Onon, Urgunge, *Mongolian Heroes of the 20th Century*, New York, 1976.
Perry-Ayscough, H.G.C. and R.B. Otter-Barry, *With the Russians in Mongolia*, London, 1914.
Price, Ernest B., *The Russo-Japanese Treaties of 1907-1916 Concerning Manchuria and Mongolia*, Baltimore, 1933.
Rupen, Robert A., *The Mongols of the Twentieth Century*, 2 vols., The Hague, 1964.
Sanjdorj, M,. *Manchu Chinese Colonial Rule in Northern Mongolia*, London, 1980.
Snow, Edgar, *Glory and Bondage*, London, 1944.
Tan, Tennyson, *The Political Status of Mongolia*, Shanghai, 1932.
Tang, Peter S.H., *Russian and Soviet Policy in Manchuria and Outer Mongolia, 1911-1931*, Durham, N.C., 1959.
Vernadsky, George, *The Mongols and Russia*, New Haven, 1953.
Vladimirtsov, B.J., *Life of Chinggis Khan*, London, 1930; trans. from Russian, Moscow, 1922.

INDEX

Abdali/Durrani, 1
Abdulla Jan, 4
Abdur Rahman, Amir, 6-10
Adrianople, 2
Afghan-Soviet agreement (1950) 33
Afghan-Soviet border commission (1946), 26
Afghan-Soviet treaty of friendship (1921), 23-24, 51
Afghan Soviet treaty (1978), 46
Afghan-Soviet treaty of neutrality and non-aggression (1926), 29
Afghan-Soviet treaty of naturalety and non-aggression (1931), 30, 33
Afro-Asian Conference (1956), 35
Ahmad Shah, founder of Modern Afghnistan, 1
Alexander, Tsar, 2
Ali Ahmad Khan, Sardar, 10
Amin, Hafizullah, 40
Amursana/Amursanang, 12, 13
Anglo-Afghan peace treaty (1919), 10
Anglo-Afghan war (1139-42), 2
Anglo-Russian boundary commission (1875), 7
Anglo-Russian boundary protocol (1887), 7
Anglo-Russian convention (1907), 9
Ayub Khan, Sardar, 5, 6, 9

Babar, Zahiruddin Muhammad, Emperor, 28
Babrak Karmal, 43, 47
BBC (Brittsh Broadcasting Corporation), 68
Bacha-i-Sakka, 6, 41
Basmachi, 25
Bata, Sanjiin, 63
Bismark, Prince, 5
Bogdo, 20, 78

Bogdo Khan, 13, 17
Boxer movement, 13
Brezhnev, L. I., 41, 42, 46, 65, 67
Buddhism, 11
Bukhara, 25
Bulganin, N.A., 34, 64, 65

CENTO (Central Treaty Organization), 34
Chakdorzhav, D., 51
Chakhundorj, *Tushetu Khan*, 11
Chengun, Zasaghtu Khan, 13
Chernenko, Konstantin, 45, 70
Ch'en Yi, Marshal, 40
Chiang Kai-shek, 56, 66
Ch'ien Lung, Emperor, 12, 46
Chimiddorj, D., 63
Chinese-Mongolian agreement (1952), 60, 70
Chinese-Mongolian boundary treaty (1962), 70
Chinese-Mongolian consular treaty (1986), 70
Chinese-Mongolian-Russian treaty (1915), 17
Chinese-Russian declaration (1913), 17
Chinese-Russian rivalry, 13
Chinese-Russian treaty (1727), 13
Chinese-Soviet treaty(1924), 55 (1945), 57
Chinggis Khan, 61, 62
Chinggis Khan Temple, 61
Chitral, 7
Choibalson, Kho, 51
Churchill, Winston S., 56
CMEA (Council on Mutual Assistance), 35
Communism, 25
Communist Party of China (CPC), 55, 67

Communist Party of Soviet Union (CCCPSU), 62
Congress of Berlin, 4
Crimean Conference, 31
Cultural Revolution, 60, 61, 65

Dawi, Abdul Hadi, 26
Doksom. D., 51
Dost Muhammad Khan, Amir, 49
Dufferin, Lord, 7
Dulles, John Foster, 34

East India Company, 4, 31
Eisenhower, President Dwight D., 36

Far Eastern Republic, 20
Fiyanggu, Commander, 12
Fotress of Asia, 49
Ford, President Gerald, 67

Galdan, *Boshoghtu Khan*, 11-12
Germany, 9
Germany-Turkish mission, 9
Golden Horde, 62
Gorbachev, Mikhail S., 46, 72
Great Wall of China, 10, 16

Habibullah, a Tajik brigand, 6
Habibullah Khan. Amir, 8-9
Homaira. Queen, 36
Hsu Shu-ts'ang 19, 52

Ilychev, L.P., 62
Indian Ocean, 49,
Indian revolutionary(ies), 9
Indonesia, 11
Inner Mongolia/Inner Mongolian Autonomous Region (IMAR), 11, 15, 18
Islamic Conference 43, 44

Jagvaral, Nyamyn, 63
Jamal Khan, 1
Jebtsundamba, 12, 13

Kalgi Avatar, 14

Kalinin, M.I., 23, 46
K'ang,hsi, Emperor, 11-12
Kashgaria, 13
Khailier pass, 48
Khiva, 25
Khural, 54
Khrushchev, N.S., 34, 63, 64, 65
Konstatinovich Zukhov, Georgi', 56
Kosich, D.I., 51
Kwangtung army, 54

Lenin, V.I., 23-24
Ligdan Khan, 11
Losel, D., 5
Lytton. Lord, 5

Mahendra Pratap, 9
Malalai, 6
Manchu-Kuo, 54
Manchuria, 13, 17, 54
Mao Tse-tung/Mao Zedong, 55, 64
Mayo, Lord, 4
Mohammed Ali Khan, Sardar, 10
Mohammed Aziz Khan, 10
Mohammed Barakatullah, 9
Mohammed Daoud Khan, Sardar, 34
Mohammed Hashim Khan, Sardar, 10
Mohammed Nadir Khan, Sardar, 10
Mohammed Naim, 38
Mohammed Zahir Khan, Shah, 29
Mongolian Revolution, 68
Mongolian-Soviet pact (1936), 56, 57
Mongolian-Soviet trade agreement (1923), 52
Mongolian-Soviet treaty (1946), 57, 66
Mongolian-Soviet treaty (1966), 66, 67
Muhammad Afzal Khan, Sardar and Amir, 5
Muhammad Yusuf Khan, Sardar, 6, 10, 41
Mujahidin(s) 41

Najibullah, 46
Napoleon I, Emperor, 2
Neratov, 14
Nesselrode, K.V., 2
Nikolai II, Tsar, 14

Index

North-West Frontier of India, 8

Outer Mongolia, 17-18

Pacific Ocean, 11
Pahlavi, Shah Mohammed Reza, 37-38
Paikes, A.K., 52
Panjab, 2, 3
Payinda Khan, 1
Persian Gulf, 49
Peter the Great, Tsar, 12
Petrov, A.O., 51
Petrov, Ivan, 13
Podgorny, Nikolai, 37-38
Poland, 11, 67
Pol Pot regime, 69

Raskolnikov, F.P., 25
Reagan, President Ronald, 46
Renmin Ribao, 61
Roosevelt, President Franklin D. 56
RSFSR, 23
Russo-Japanese agreement(s), 17
Russo-Mongol agreement (1912), 16-17, 52
Russo-Turkish War (1877-78), 4

Saadabad pact, 30
Said Mir Alim, Emir, 25
SAVAK, 37
Semenov, Ataman Grigori, 20
Shagdarsuren, P., 63
Shah Mahmud Khan, Sardar, 10
Sher Ali Khan, Amir, 4-5
Shuja-ul-Mulk, Shah, 2-4
Sino-Soviet treaty, 53
Siraj-ul-Akhbar-i-Afghaniya, 9
Snow, Edgar, 55
Sorkin, N.S., 51
Sosorbaram, S., 63
Sri Vijaya, 11

Stalin, J.V., 54, 56, 57, 60, 64
Stoletov, General G.N., 4
Super Power summit(s), 46

Taraki, Nur Muhammad, 39
Tarzi, Mahmud Beg, 9
Teb Tengri, Mongolshaman, 10
Temujin. *Chinggis Khan*, 10-11
Temur Ochir, D., 62
Tibet, 11
Timur Shah, 2
Toghon Temur Shun Ti, 11
Tsedenbal, Yu, 60-64, 67-68, 71
Tuvan People's Republic, 55

Ulan Bator, 55
Unen, newspaper, 67
Ungern-Sternberg, 20-21
Utai, 18

Vasilyevich Chicherin, Georgi, 53

Wakhan, 7
White Tsar, 14
World War I, 10
World War II, 57

Xinjiang/Sinkiang, 18, 73, 74

Yahya Khan, Sardar, 6
Yakub Khan, Amir, 7, 9
Yalta agreement, 64
Yousuf, Mohammed, 36
Yuan dynasty, 17
Yuan Li, 52
Yuan Shi-kai, 17

Zaman Shah, 2, 3
Zedong, Mao, 71
Zhou Enlai, 40, 59, 61, 63, 64, 67
Zulfiqar Pass, 7